THE LAST VOYAGE OF TH—

OLIVE\

1938 to 1٩

From the original log written by

Len Townend

Edited by Elvin Carter

Blue Elvan Books

Published 2010 by Blue Elvan Books

35 Tremayne Close, Devoran, Truro, Cornwall. TR3 6QE

Typeset by Marie Bird of Devoran

4, Carnon Mine, Devoran, Truro, Cornwall. TR3 6NG

ISBN 978 0 9559950-1-9

Printed and bound in Great Britain by BoothPrint

The Praze, Penryn, Cornwall. TR10 8AA

Sailplan of a four masted barque

Bowsprit Sails	Foremast sails	Mainmast staysails
1. Flying jib 2. Outer jib 3. Inner jib 4. Fore topmast staysail	5. Foresail or course 6. Fore lower topsail 7. Fore upper topsail 8. Fore lower topgallant 9. Fore upper topgallant 10. Fore royal	11. Main topgallant staysail 12. Main topmast staysail 13. Main royal staysail
Mainmast sails	**Mizzenmast Staysails**	**Mizzen mast sails**
14. Mainsail or course 15. Main lower topsail 16. Main upper topsail 17. Main lower topgallant 18. Main upper topgallant 19. Main royal	20. Mizzen topgallant staysail 21. Mizzen topmast staysail 22. Mizzen royal staysail	23. Crossjack or crojack 24. Mizzen lower topsail 25. Mizzen upper topsail 26. Mizzen lower topgallant 27. Mizzen upper topgallant 28. Mizzen royal
Jiggermast staysails	**Jigger or Gaff sails**	
29. Jigger staysail 30. Jigger middle staysail 31. Jigger topmast staysail	32. Gaff or spanker topsail 33. Jigger driver or spanker	

Editors Acknowledgements.

Firstly my thanks to Sue Earle (Townend) and her sisters for allowing me to publish this fine account of their father's voyage.

Secondly to Marie Bird who has once again typeset this book at a time of great personal tragedy with the loss of her husband Ralph; shipwright, world renowned Pilot Gig builder and friend. Thanks are hardly adequate to express how grateful I am.

Thanks to Thomas 'Walker' Simpson MBE (2002) Deputy Coxswain/ Mechanic of the Lifeboat at Donaghadee, Northern Ireland for the photographs of his father Tom on his boat 'Miss Dorothy'.

Also to Jeff Yates of Newcastle N.S.W. Australia for his photographs of his Grandfather Fred Boy (who sadly passed away on 6th Dec 2009 aged 94) and the wheat ketch Falie.

To my Brother-in Law Jon Robertshaw who first set me in motion with the wonderful logs of his uncle Geoffrey Robertshaw in my first book and for letting me use some of the photographs again.

To the late Derrick Dean of Andrew Weir and Co. Ltd. his widow Gill.and to a host of others far too numerous to record, my sincere thanks to you all for your interest and encouragement.

The photographs in this book have been taken from Len's album and I have most of the negatives, all attempts have been made to locate any others. As sailors swap photographs regularly, Geoffrey Robertshaw was very free with his vast collection, I can only say that there has been no attempt to lay claim to them but only use them to augment the reader's involvement in a wonderful story and offer my apologies to any original owners.

Last words. To my family who have put up with my over enthusiasm for the subject, thank you and you may now yawn openly.

Introduction

Born in 1917 in Hartshead Len Townend was a true merchant seaman and was around ships and shipping and sailor men from his earliest days in Bridlington. In 1947 Len met and married Margaret Gibson and they had four daughters Ruth, Anne, Sue and Jane. It was after the birth of Ruth that Len decided to 'come ashore' in the early 1950's and quit the seafaring life to become a long distance lorry driver. Before he passed away in 1998 Len typed up his recollections of this, his only commercial trip under sail, from his original rough logs.

This is a great book.

Within these pages is a story in every sense of the word. It has a beginning, full of hope and some trepidation, a middle, with the feeling of achievement and exhilaration and an end that is poignant and tragic.

It is a true and factual account of the last voyage of the sailing vessel Olivebank as seen from the deck, from aloft and from the fo'c'sle by a man who made that voyage. A man who was proud to have taken part in the Last Great Grain Race in 1938-1939 and like Eric Newby is telling it 'as it was' with all the humour and the hardship.

There were 13 ships in that last race and though the Moshulu with Eric Newby onboard was the eventual winner, there are still good tales to be told on board the other twelve and every sailor loves a good tale.

So, if you are ready to sit and let the lamp swing you are in for a really great story and though the ships were 'tall' and some of the stories even taller this one is the truth and will hold you to the last page.

Elvin Carter Devoran March 2010

Acknowledgments

I owe much to Captain Carl Granith and the officers and crew of 'OLIVEBANK' for teaching me my job.

I also owe much to Skipper J.F. Hill of Fleetwood and to Frank (Honest Tom) Pepper who served as bosun in Furness lines for well over 30 years.

To Skipper Frank (Willy) Tallentire owner of the motor cable 'BLUE JACKET' of Bridlington.

To Skipper Tom Hutchinson who was for many years coxswain of the Bridlington lifeboat and to all those other old hands who through the years educated me in the ways of the sea.

Sadly now many are no longer with us, but I am grateful to them all and it was my good fortune and privilege to have known them and I consider that my life was enriched by having sailed with them all.

Len Townend

SAILING VESSEL OLIVEBANK

Four masted barque built 1892 by

Messers Mackie & Thomson.

(Glasgow)

Dimensions given as Length 326'

Breadth 43'1" Depth 24'5"

Registry No. 99855

Flag code MTFW

According to my discharge certificate she was 2795 Gross, 2427 Net. According to Gustaf Erikson's letter head she was 4,400 tons deadweight and had capacity for 1,300 standards. As of 1938 she rated No.5 in size of the Erikson fleet of 14 sailing vessels.

MOSHULU 5,000 tons Dead Weight.

PASSAT 4,700 tons Dead Weight.

LAWHILL 4,600 tons Dead Weight.

PAMIR 4,500 tons Dead Weight.

'OLIVEBANK' was one of the latter day big carriers, to some degree a trifle slab sided, as no doubt all the big ones were, but she was a beautiful vessel to behold from a distance of a mile or so, as she had a really good sheer which did much to enhance her appearance. She had a raised fo'c'sle head and poop and the main deck stretched from one to the other in an unbroken line with no Liverpool House to spoil these lines. In heavy weather the disadvantage of one long open deck, being that when you shipped a big sea, it thundered down the deck with little to stop it.

I did not see all the Erikson fleet, but to me at least 'OLIVEBANK' had the finest appearance of any square rigger that I have seen. (No doubt crew members of other ships in the fleet would contest this statement). I saw most of the fleet and as a lad I had seen many big vessels off Flamborough Head and in later years it was my good fortune to see several others as I tramped around the globe.

In the last 3 decades or so of commercial sail the vessels were sold relatively cheaply, as by now there was little demand for them.

It was often said that a brand new suit of sails would cost as much to purchase as would the vessel to set them on.

'OLIVEBANK' carried royal yards and in all could carry (as I recall) 31 sails, she could have carried 33 sails if she had set Royal stay sails from main and mizzen plus jigger topgallant staysail but I only recollect her carrying 18 square sails, 4 head sails, spanker and spanker gaff topsail, main and mizzen topmast and topgallant staysails and 3 staysails from the jigger mast.

The lower masts were constructed of steel and stepped into the keelson and at main deck level would be at least 3 feet in diameter and probably a little in excess of this.

The mainmast would be in the region of 190 feet from truck to keelson and the main yard in excess of 90 feet in length. (Should anyone have the exact measurements I shall be happy to be corrected.)

'Olive' the finest figurehead in the fleet.

STARTING AT THE FO'C'SLE HEAD
AND WORKING TO THE POOP.

The lower anchors were always stowed on the fo'c'sle head when at sea, the chain cables unshackled and stowed, and plugs put into the hawse pipes.

On the fo'c'sle head was the largest capstan in the ship, with 2 sets of holes into which the wooden capstan bars could be inserted. Using the lower set of holes and tramping anti-clockwise was single gear. With the bars in the upper set of holes and tramping clockwise the capstan was working in double gear.

This capstan had many uses including warping, handling the anchor inboard and outboard etc. It could also be coupled up to the windlass, which was positioned under the fo'c'sle head. Seldom was steam, used to raise the anchor as coal would be much more expensive than man-power.

It was said that one and a half revolutions of the capstan in double gear raised one link of the anchor cable.

I never got the chance to check this one out, as I was always fully employed trying to wear a path in the deck planking round the capstan with my feet but if we had eight or nine shackles out it was a long hard sweat getting that anchor broken out.

Situated on the fo'c'sle head were also the port and starboard navigation lights, each set in a little round tower standing about 3 feet high.

Under the fo'c'sle head were entrance hatches to the forepeak and chain locker and a separate hatch into the coal bunker, coal being for galley stove and donkey boiler only. (We did not possess any such refinements as a bogey stove in either of the fo'c'sles where we had our accommodation, nor for that matter were there any in the poop.) In the middle of this space was a windlass and ranged down each side, several lockers.

Bosun's locker, for small bits and pieces.

Potato locker.

Crew's washroom. No showers in those days, just a galvanized tank to soak dirty clothes in and a low wooden bench on which you rested your bucket when you took a bath.

The pig pen was immediately abaft the washroom on the port side. Opposite was the crew's loo, or Head, which by modern standards left much to be desired. It consisted of a plank with a hole in it, underneath which was a metal funnel leading into a soil pipe and thence out through the ships side. In bad weather this was a most uncomfortable place to be, for you were well forward and getting the worst of the weather as the old ship rolled and lifted and dived. Diving being the greatest problem, for the clack valve at the outboard end of the soil pipe was either seized in the open position or else non-existent and whilst not wishing to make too fine a point of it, the effects could be devastating for the poor unfortunate sitting there if the ship dived at the wrong moment.

Abaft the break of the fo'c'sle head was the small No. 1 hatch, the foremast, water tanks for washing purposes and then the forward deck house, or fo'c'sle, which accommodated 12 hands.

In a separate section at the after end of this compartment was the donkey boiler and winch with a warping drum protruding from each side of the house. On the port side drum was also a gipsy which could be coupled by a light chain to another gipsy on the windlass to give steam power to the latter.

On top of this deck house were stowed the motor boat and the 'pram' which was a handy boat for rowing and working over the side at water level when in Port.

Next came No. 2 hatch, mainmast, brace winches, (hand operated) and the galley, which had on top the only other steam winch.

Then came No.3 hatch, mizzen mast, bilge pump (hand operated of course but unfortunately not in use owing to a cracked suction pipe) brace winches and then what we called the after fo'c'sle, but what in reality would be the apprentices half deck. It housed six of us in the fore part (as there were no apprentices on this trip) and in the after part in 2 separate sections were housed the carpenter and sail maker, bosun (boatswain) and donkey man known as the 'idlers'. This not being strictly true as they worked as hard as anyone else and had to go aloft if required, we even had the steward and cook up there on the odd occasion when we had a real hard blow.

On top of this deck house was the standard compass with a flying bridge connecting up with that 'holy of holies' the poop. On either side of this deck house were situated the 2 life boats, davits, skids and chocks, and abaft the deck house was the small No.4 hatch and then the break of the poop.

On the poop was the mizzen brace winch, saloon skylight, chart house with access to the saloon and then the steering compass and the large steering wheel. The steering wheel (helm) had 10 spokes and was about 6 feet across its diameter from spoke tip to spoke tip.

'OLIVEBANK' had only a single wheel, unlike some of the vessels which carried two, one set behind the other. With the latter type four men were sometimes at the wheel together in bad weather. With our single wheel, two men steered in bad weather, with help from the Officer of the watch when things got a bit hectic.

No steam steering engine here, no electric tele-motor or new fangled push button device, just brute force, a worm gear and rope relieving tackles - and that wheel sure could kick. It has thrown more than one man over the top, and I have been halfway over myself.

The steering gear was right aft, and the helmsman and steering gear were sheltered by a fairly large whaleback which gave one a lot of protection from the weather and following seas.

Inside the poop was the accommodation for the Captain, deck officers, steward and cook. There was a saloon and store rooms for the food, which was kept at all times under lock and key, also the sail makers' work-room was under the starboard side. Below decks, abaft the bulk head was the LAZARET which was very spacious and was used for the sail locker and storage of paints, etc.

Between the forward and after bulk heads was the one big hold running full length. It was served by the four hatches and contained the domestic water tank which ran from tween deck to deck head and was quite a large tank. Strictly speaking what was often called the tween deck was in actual fact also termed as being the main deck and or the lower deck, with regards to 'Ship Construction'.

On 'OLIVEBANK' this deck was always referred to as the mellom (middle) deck.

'OLIVEBANK' had what may be termed a skeletal tween deck with very little plating though as I recall there was some plating around the hatch coamings (deck beam tie plates) and masts. Four plated catwalks 2ft wide ran fore and aft, one each side of the coamings and one each side of the tween decks close up to the frames (deck stringers) also a little plating close to the two bulkheads and the rest was just the ships beams.

Many of these old ships must have gone down like stones when they got holed. They were truly, coffin ships.

Olivebank

THE ACCOMMODATION

The fo'c'sle had 12 bunks, lockers for oilskins, clothes, and seamen's gear, water tank, food and crockery locker, the crockery being of the tin mug and enamel ware variety.

There was a large table and two wooden benches of the same length running fore and aft.

I think there were two oil lamps, but only one would be allowed to be used at sea and that would have to be turned down very low after about 2100 hours as oil was very precious and in short supply. It would cost about one shilling and three pence (12p) a gallon in the U.K. at that time and cheaper if you bought it in bulk but there was no margin for waste in the Erikson fleet.

Several sea chests were scattered about on which one could sit but no bogey stove or any means of keeping warm and of course no-where to dry wet clothes.

In bad weather it didn't seem to matter, as everything was wet anyway and one just kept the lot on and on several occasions we turned in 'all standing' sea boots, oilskins and all.

No time to start getting dressed if the mate blew 3 blasts on his whistle calling out all hands but what did it matter? We were young and tough, we were hard cases. At least, that was the image we tried to project and by the Grace of God we took little harm.

The fo'c'sle had one big skylight and in the after end of it was a beautiful painting of the 'OLIVEBANK', painted a few years earlier by that very well known marine artist Claude Muncaster, when he made a voyage in her.

This painting was a very much prized work and was shown to most all those who visited the ship and it was always kept bright and clean, and of course is illustrated in Mr. Muncaster's fine book, "Rolling round the Horn", which is his own account of a voyage in 'OLIVEBANK'.

Olivebank becalmed

Editors note. I do not know if the photograph included is of the painting in question but it certainly appears in Mr Muncasters book and yet I have the negative.

Our fo'c'sle housed six of us with the same type of fitments as for'ard, it would have less than half the cubic space of the 12 berth but was probably a little more cosy. However, we only had one oil lamp and if we didn't turn it low at about 2100 hrs we were rather vulnerable, as the officer on the watch would notice the brightness of the light through the skylight when he came to look at the standard compass. Then with much swearing and stomping of feet we were told to turn it low. We sometimes thought they only came to look at the skylight and not the bloody compass.

The P.O.'s accommodation was small and very cramped 2 double berth cabins and 2 small but separate mess rooms. The bunk boards and the fittings were of polished wood whereas they were painted in the 2 fo'c'sles, but the P.O.'s had no other refinements in their cabins.

The bunks for all hands other than the after guard, were simply painted wooden boards to lie on and a bunk board running the length of the bunk to stop you rolling, out. If you required a mattress, pillow, blankets, eating and drinking utensils, bucket and other such comforts you provided your own. This of course was common practice with many of the British and European shipping lines right up to the late 1930's. I was never provided with sheets, pillow cases and counterpane until I sailed with Furness Withy from Feb 1940.

I well remember striking up a conversation with a Belgian seaman on the platform at Cardiff station the day I paid off 'OLIVEBANK' on the 15th of August, 1939. He had just left a ship and was heading home for Antwerp complete with all his gear, a sea bag, tattered suit case, pillow rolled up in his 'donkeys breakfast' (mattress) and his bucket. I couldn't help thinking, my God it is time we were emancipated. Happily, in later years we were, but it took a war.

This fine model of Olivebank was made by the Rev Alston of Veryan,Cornwall in 1936 and can still be seen there.

The connection is unknown.

Thanks to Derrick Dean for the information. Ed.

THE FOOD

In 'OLIVEBANK' we were thrice blessed. Firstly we had a really good Steward. Secondly, we had an equally good Cook and both he and the Steward were spotlessly clean. The galley and its contents shone at all times and one had to be a very privileged person indeed to cross over that storm sill. Thirdly, as we made average passages out and home there was never any real shortage of food.

We did not of course have a fridge or even an ice box, so fresh meat and fish only lasted a day or two and with the exception of root vegetables - we soon ran out of fresh food as the green vegetables did not last very long.

We had to empty the potato locker fairly frequently, throw away the bad ones, and those that the rats had nibbled and then de-sprout the remainder. Once the potatoes were finished we carried some tinned ones and some potato flour (for mashed potato) and then fell back on to rice as a substitute.

As in most ships of that time you could tell the hour of the day, and the day of the week by the food being dished up. Often we moaned about the food to each other - what seaman didn't in those days - for there used to be a saying, "the better you were, fed, the better was your pay", which to some degree was quite true.

Looking back I feel we were quite well fed under the circumstances and certainly no one on that voyage suffered from malnutrition and though some of us may have looked a bit lean, at least we were fit and active.

I once fared worse on a hard case North Yorkshire coal burning tramp SS 'SCORESBY' Headlam Steam Ship Company of Whitby. We came home from the River Plate and spent Christmas 1939 in Avonmouth. Christmas dinner was Liverpool Scouse no less. This surely would not be the fault of the owners but rather a lack of imagination by the catering department.

At the other end of the food scale was being on the Whaler SS 'BRANSFIELD' United Whalers, London, where there was no strict rationing and where the cost of food per man per voyage must have been astronomical. I saw men come off the night shift, when we were on the whaling grounds, and pack away five or six beef steaks, pork chops, liver and whatever.

In 'OLIVEBANK' we always had beautiful fresh bread made daily and sweet bread rolls which contained a lot of condensed milk were also made fresh daily and eaten at both morning and afternoon smokes. I can still smell that bread baking and the coffee brewing as I write this down, a lovely aroma indeed. Seldom were we given hard tack and when we were it didn't contain many, if any, weevils. We only ever had hard tack in extremely bad weather, when it made cooking and baking very difficult but we never went without one hot meal a day.

Several times we caught fish whilst at sea. Bonito which were called 'Springers' by the crew and which made beautiful eating. Shark, which I think I only ate once, it is very coarse, oily and strong in flavor. Also various other fish which included a lot of long snouted Gar Fish which we caught in the Spencer Gulf while laying at anchor. We also had a very tasty dish from time to time called 'Lever Lada' the main ingredients being liver, rice and currents. I enjoyed this dish very much and also another favourite of mine 'Speke Sild' diced raw salt herring which needs to have been at least six weeks in salt, chopped onion and pickling spices soaked over night in a solution of vinegar and water. Potatoes were nearly always served up boiled in their jackets but on occasions were served fried, along with fried onions and corned beef.

Pea soup was usually very thick with chunks of pork in it.

Barley pudding was similar to rice just substituting rice for barley.

Lapskois.or Lobskous or Lapskous was a form of dry hash, a corruption of this being our own 'Scouse' which as I knew it was wet or a form of Irish Stew.

Tinned meat balls and tinned fish balls were also served once in a while also tinned sausages. Fresh vegetables were served with meat and potatoes while stocks lasted and fried onions which happily lasted for much of the voyage out.

We had meat every day as far as I can recall, and sometimes twice and even three times on occasion. Mostly the meat was salt beef and pork and of course corned beef and as we carried three live pigs on the outward leg of the journey to Australia, we had fresh meat every once in a while.

Chippy, Kaiko Luotonen and the Steward, Arno Stromberg used to perform the execution and then we were served pork nearly every meal until the pig was all eaten. The pigs were slaughtered in a humane way. Firstly they were stunned and then bled which was the practice adopted ashore in those days. There was no cruelty or brutality just a job quickly and cleanly performed. The cook used to catch most of the blood, which was mixed with flour or oatmeal and made into blood pudding pancakes about four inches in diameter and about half an inch thick and tasted much like the black puddings one buys in the shops and were very tasty indeed.

Whilst in South Australia a similar practice prevailed, only this time we took live sheep aboard and so we had mutton and more mutton.

Cook Rolf Forsman

19

A typical week's menu

	BREAKFAST	DINNER	TEA
SUN	Macaroni & Pork	Meat, Potatoes Stewed Apricots & Milk	Meat & Potatoes
MON	Rice & Curry	Thick Pea Soup. Pancakes & Jam	Meat & Potatoes
TUES	Porridge & Milk Corned Beef	Salt Beef & Potatoes Mixed Stewed Fruit	Meat & Potatoes
WED	Beans & Meat	Stockfish & Potatoes Barley Pudding	Fried Meat & Potatoes
THUR	Porridge, Milk Corned Beef	Meat Soup (Wet Hash) & Cocoa	Dry Hash (Lapskaus)
FRI	Rice & Curry	Pea Soup Pancakes & Jam	Meat & Potatoes
SAT	Beans & Meat	Meat & Potatoes Mixed Stewed Fruit	Rice, Apricot Pudding & Milk

THE LANGUAGE

Finnish and Swedish, were the two languages spoken, with of course some English.

Finland had at one time been under Swedish dominance and so around the Aland Islands and mainland coastal Finland, Swedish was the spoken language. However, in some cases Finnish was spoken, so, here was the rather odd situation of Finnish nationals unable to converse freely with one another.

As I recall, Chippy, Sail maker and Donkey man all used Finnish and spoke very little, if any, Swedish.

Adrian Seligman says in his book "there is little or no language barrier amongst ships mixed crews, as once you have been in close proximity for a short while an understanding seems to develop."

One could call it the language of the sea I suppose.

I have sailed both as an A.B. and as a bosun with many men from foreign parts and it has never been too long before I could understand them and they me, in a limited way. I do not speak any foreign language fluently. I don't even profess to speak the Queens English correctly, but I can get by in most parts of Scandinavia. Probably one reason for this was that I was brought up, more or less, within the fishing community of Bridlington and in those days, though not so much now, the local dialect of the fisher folk and agricultural workers had been much influenced by the language of the Vikings and Norsemen who had raided and settled in those parts. This meant that many of the words in daily use were, in some cases, identical both in pronunciation and meaning to the words used by the Scandinavians on board. So happily for me, I soon picked up enough words to be able to converse, after a fashion.

I still write to and visit an old whaling pal of mine in Norway and he also to me, in what his wife who speaks and writes very good English calls Chinese-English. Many people may not understand it but I think most West European seamen could.

Most of the Erikson vessels appeared to carry one or two British men, though I do not think there was any hard and fast ruling on this and as the fleet usually discharged its cargoes in the United Kingdom, there would never be any shortage of applicants to fill what few vacancies existed.

I understand that in those days a reasonable command of the English language was required before one could sit the examination for 2nd Mate in the Nautical Academies' of Finland, so no doubt we British contributed just a little more than "heave ho" man power during those voyages.

It was very noticeable that after learning just a few of the basic words - i.e. knife, fork, spoon, etc. one seemed to swing over very rapidly to all the "cuss" words. And it was truly remarkable just how soon one became fluent and proficient in this field and many is the time we have had a swearing session with each other and we surely did put a lot of feeling into it.

Such was our mentality or rather lack of it.

A fine body of men, self 2ⁿᵈ on left Geoff far right.

S/V OLIVEBANK.   MARIEHAMN.   1938 - 1939.
LEFT GLASGOW   OCT: 22$^{\underline{nd}}$ ARRIVED PORT VICTORIA.
SOUTH AUSTRALIA FEB: 2$^{\underline{nd}}$ 1939.
DEPARTED PORT VICTORIA MARCH 20$^{\underline{TH}}$ 1939.
ARRIVED QUEENSTOWN FOR ORDERS JULY 17$^{\underline{TH}}$ 1939.
DISCHARGED CARGO AT BARRY DOCK JULY-AUGUST 1939.
OLIVEBANK SUNK BY GERMAN MINE IN NORTH SEA 8/9/39.

CAPTAIN CARL GRANITH.   MASTER.

R. VUORI. 1$^{\underline{ST}}$ MATE. K. ANDERSSON. 2$^{\underline{ND}}$ MATE. O. POLLONEN. 3$^{\underline{RD}}$ MATE.

PORT WATCH.   **STARBOARD WATCH.**
                                              SAIL MAKER.
CARPENTER. *Kaiku Luotonen*   *Niila Kango*
            Tor Sontag   *Arthur Evert Blomqvist*
            Ule Kanewa   *Olof Forstén*
            Erter Berndtson   *Pär Finneman.*
            [signature]   *Julius Henriksson.*
            Albin Björkman.   *Sam Johansson.*
            Gunnar Lindroos   *Lennart Henriksson*
            [signature]   *Valter England.*
DONKEY MAN. MAKINEN.   *Arne Laakso.*
            G.S. ROBERTSHAW.   *Leonard. H. Townend.*

            Arno Strömberg STEWARD.
            Rolf Forsman   COOK.

THE SHIPS COMPLEMENT

Some of the crew Ragnar at centre rear.

The full complement consisted of Master, 1st Mate, 2nd Mate, 3rd Mate, Steward, Cook, Carpenter, Boatswain, Sail maker and Donkey man, plus 18 hands in the fo'c'sles that is to say, Able seamen, Ordinary seamen and Deck boys.

A total ships compliment of 28 men and boys.

We sailed 2 men short from Glasgow, namely the bosun and one sea man which reduced us to 26. On the voyage home there was a further reduction of two more, as we had to leave the Donkey man in hospital and also a seaman left us in Australia.

So, on the homeward run we were only 24.

No union rules here, therefore no short hand money was forthcoming.

The crew, were great shipmates and I was accorded much kindness throughout the voyage by each and every member. I can still envisage their appearances and something of their character, or at least the ways of each and every one. A good crowd of lads, hardworking and easy going and for the most part placid enough and though we had our differences as, obviously we must, I never once saw a blow struck in anger aboard the ship.

Ashore was a different matter, when old scores with lads off other ships were sometimes settled, usually after a few pints.

Working conditions under normal workaday circumstances were too hard for the most part. We were always kept at it with some job or other but as long as we did our best and jumped to it when it was necessary, we were never chased around or hazed in any way

Work on deck

Captain Carl Granith

CAPTAIN CARL GRANITH (Editors note. Standing next to a lady that I think is Isabella Kiernander the poet) was a great shipmaster, as those windjammer men had to be, he was also a man's man and a gentleman. I feel also that he was a great humanitarian and looking back I think I would have followed him anywhere. He commanded great respect and though strictly a no nonsense type of person he got discipline and respect from all those serving under his command without having to raise his voice. He was a fairly big man with a kindly face, often to be seen on the poop taking his exercise in carpet slippers. Probably for two reasons:

(I) They would no doubt be very comfortable.

(2) He would not wish to disturb those sleeping in the cabins below.

He had a deep voice which could be heard above the wind when he gave commands down in the roaring forties, but otherwise seldom raised his voice unless something really displeased him.

Rumour had it that on a previous voyage in one of the ships he had successfully operated on 2 crew members who each had appendicitis. However, I cannot substantiate this although I believe it to be true as I heard it from more than one source.

Once, when I was chipping rust I managed to get a fair sized piece of scale in my eye and the 'Old Man' tried to remove it with a wet handkerchief screwed up at the corner with no luck at all. We tried an eyebath but still no joy, that scale was firmly affixed, so he told me to lie flat on my back on the bench along the side of the saloon skylight. He screwed up the corner of his handkerchief once more and informing me it would most likely hurt, he poised himself and from what appeared to be a great height, he dive-bombed my eye and it sure did hurt, but he shifted that scale.

Captain Granith would never have men taking unnecessary risks.

When going up onto the poop it was customary to approach by the lee-side ladder, so that the old man, and the officers of the watch had the weather side of the poop to themselves but if she was heeling over and there was water on the main deck, the old man used to tell us to come up the weather side ladder – not always so with some of the mates!

Ragnar Wuori

RAGNAR WUORI (above) was the 1st Mate, a short stocky figure probably 5ft 6ins tall, very compact, very muscular and a great seaman.

Once he got to know you he would impart some of his knowledge, should you be sufficiently interested.

He had a twinkle in his eye and one or two gold fillings which seemed to shine when he laughed. He was a handy lad with his fists and seemed when ashore to love to have a go at someone or other.

I once saw him get his face badly pulped up in Port Victoria by a crew member off one of the other ships, who was twice as big as Ragnar. He patched up his wounds and I think it was two nights later, went ashore for a return contest but I never heard whether or not he found his man, though I feel he would have left no stone unturned, such was our mate.

Ragnar was one of only two men I have met who on occasion would, if sufficiently vexed, hurl his peaked cap to the deck and repeatedly jump on it, much to everyone's mirth, but by all the Saints never let him catch you laughing.

The other cap flattener was Skipper Billy Peck of the Manchester Ship Canal paddle tug 'Irlam'.

Ragnar Wuori was affectionately known as 'gamla a skriker' or 'old screamer'. It was said that he had served all his sea time in 'OLIVEBANK' and that he had worked his way up from deck boy to first mate in her.

This I cannot vouch for but I heard the story several times. Possibly further information might be obtained from the Erikson Line, or Karl Kahre, Alands Sjofarts Museum or Adrian Seligman.

Editors Note. According to the memorabilia of Geoffrey Robertshaw which is in my possession, Ragnar was the Donkeyman on the OLIVEBANK in 1932 when Geoff sailed in her with Adrian Seligman who was called Sam on the ships papers.

Ragnar had a phrase which he often used to we two British hands 'carefully and cleverly' he would say to us if we were going at some job or other in a bull headed manner, "Carefully and cleverly, Townend is the way to do it".

KNUT ANDERSON was the 2nd Mate, a big dark haired young man of about 27 or 28 years of age. He came from Mariehamn and as I was in his watch he was my tormentor, but only when I deserved it. He walked with his toes pointing outwards and was a very powerful man.

OLAVI POLLONEN the 3rd Mate was a pleasant lad in his mid twenties and of medium build. He was quite a handy lad as he had done a fair bit of boxing but he never threw his weight around. He often used to sing a few lines of a song he had heard Pola Negri sing in some film or other. He spoke much of the time in Finnish and swore in that language with great fervour and was commonly known as Garmla Perkele this being one of his cuss words, which only amounts to something as strong as damn.

ARNO STROMBERG was the ships steward, always clean and tidy and the only man in the ship to wear spectacles.

ROLF FORSMAN was the ships, cook a young man who could bake beautiful bread and an excellent cook.

Vaino Makinen,Kaiku Luotonen,Niilo Kangas

KAIKU LUOTONEN (centre above) was the carpenter, a great character, and one of the older members of the ships company, probably in his early forties. He had been many years in sail and spoke Finnish. We became firm friends and had very lengthy conversations in what could best be described as rubbish language but we understood each other.

NIILO KANGAS (right above) was the sail maker, a stocky fair haired boy. I think he was only 19 or 20 and an expert with a palm and needle.

VAINO MAKINEN (left above) was donkey-man. He had a piano accordion and provided us with much entertainment.

ARTUR EVERT BLOMQUIST and TOR SONTAG were the 2 senior A.B's as they had both got their 2nd mates tickets and were just getting in the remainder of their compulsory sea time in sail, after which period they could sail as 2nd Mates. The qualifying period being 24 months in Sail and until this period had been served one could not serve as a deck officer in either sail or power driven deep sea vessels under the Finnish flag.

The port watch was under the 1st Mate and the starboard watch under the 2nd Mate. These watches included the P.O's during the stormy periods of the voyage otherwise they were on day work along with several of the hands, once we were in fine weather.

The P.O's did not stand wheel tricks or lookouts and did not go aloft unless it was really necessary but were there to help handle the cordage at deck level.

Most of the foremost hands, in fact, I feel that all of them intended to sit for their tickets in due course.

The ages of the sailors varied from Artur Blomquist, who I think was the oldest at about 27, down to young Gunnar Lindross who at 17 years was the youngest on board.

The bosun on the previous voyage had been Danish, he came down on board several times whilst we were in Glasgow half hoping that the Mate had left. It would appear that they did not get on too well and he said he would not sail again if the Mate made the voyage.

The crew members came in all sizes and many of them were dark haired with swarthy complexions, in fact I would say the fair haired blue eyed Nordic types were in the minority, Geoff Robertshaw, the only other British sailor aboard and myself being two of the latter type. It would appear that the true Finn's forbears hailed from the East and I believe their origin was Mongolia many centuries ago or so they told me.

The crew then was split into two watches as follows:

PORT WATCH

Kaiku Luotonen

Tor Sontag

Unto Kanerva

Artur Berndtson

Alpo Alanen

Albin Bjorkman

Borge Kulberg

Gunnar Lindross

Geoff Robertshaw

Vaino Makinen

STARBOARD WATCH

Niilo Kangas

Artur Evert Blomquist

Olaf Forsten

Julius Henriksson

Sam Johansson

Lennart Henrikson

Valter England

Arne Laakso

Per Finneman

Len Townend

Happily long gone were the days of the crimps and shady boarding house masters. The ships now never had to look for a crew as there was nearly always a waiting list and vacancies would very readily be filled. No need now to 'shanghai' men.

These lads were, to some extent a different type of sailorman, most of them had had a reasonable education and most of all had their sights leveled on a career at sea. An Able Seaman's pay, in sail, was about 700 FINN MARKS per month, around £3-3-0 or £3.15p in modern money.

I believe that Able Seamen in Finnish ships other than the sailing vessels received a rather better rate of pay, around £4 per month but in view of having to get in a twentyfour month period in sail jobs were, to some extent at a premium, thus supply was greater than demand hence the lower rates of pay.

The normal sea watches were for ten hours and fourteen hours on alternate day's i.e.

Midnight to 0400 = 4 hours

0400 to 0800 = 4 hours

0800 to 1300 = 5 hours

1300 to 1900 = 6 hours

1900 to 2400 = 5 hours

Thus in a 48 hour period watch keepers got a complete change-round.

The ships normal duties and maintenance work would be carried out between the hours of 0600 to 1800 by both watch keepers and day men, often ceasing at coffee time Saturday afternoon, with usual time off for meals in the case of day men.

Watch keepers took their meals immediately before going on watch or immediately after coming off.

During the night time watches in good weather all but the helmsman, look-out and policeman (standby man) could turn in but at all times had to be ready to turn out if the officer of the watch blew two blasts on his whistle calling out the watch, or three blasts, calling out all hands.

Often in bad weather and sometimes when 'wearing ship' or 'tacking' it would be a job for all hands and men may end up working 18 or 20 hours in the day. No overtime was paid for this as this was considered to be the normal working of the ship.   Overtime was paid for some of the jobs done in port but this was often worked out on a time off in lieu basis.

I apologise for any mistakes with regard to the spelling of the crew members names. I have endeavored to spell them correctly, but there may be one or two minor errors.

The Mate's name is spelt 'WUORI' and pronounced 'VOORI' as the Scandinavians pronounce V as W and W as V. i.e.

'OLIVEBANK' was pronounced 'OLIWERBANK or 'OLEEWERBANK'.

'WINTERHUDE' was pronounced 'VINTERHUDEE'

'VIKING' was pronounced 'WEEKING'

'LAWHILL' was pronounced 'LAVHILL'

THE SLOP CHEST

The ships slop chest contained only very limited supplies of items which were all very cheap to purchase. Soap, matches, pipe tobacco and 'Dobblemans' best shag tobacco for making cigarettes, the duty free price of the latter being 7½ d per 4oz packet which amounts to around 3½ pence in today's money.

THE OUTWARD VOYAGE TO AUSTRALIA

Geoff Robertshaw on the left and self

Geoff Robertshaw was an old hand at serving in windjammers having made three previous voyages during the 1930's in the Erikson fleet.

He had served in 'OLIVEBANK' on a previous voyage and had served under Captain Granith in 'PONAPE' and also one voyage in 'WINTERHUDE'.

As Geoff and I lived only a few miles from each other we said our farewells and took the train from Bradford to Glasgow one Saturday afternoon in Mid October 1938.

We reported aboard at 1830hrs on that same evening of the 15th, October, 1938 and were duly shown to our quarters where we met up with the four crew members Borje Kulberg, Albin Bjorkman, Arne Laakso and Gunnar Lindross; all first trippers in sail like myself. We six were to share the quarters for the voyage and happily we all became good friends.

Sunday 16/10/1938.

Geoff took me out on deck and commenced to show me the ropes or I should say lines, and we went up aloft and lay out on the upper tops'l yard and then went as far up as the upper to'gallant and from this vantage point it looked a long way down to the deck.

We went aloft

The lower rigging and shrouds took one up as far as the main yard and futtocks and then to get over the futtocks and onto the tops one had to go up several ratlines leaning out at an angle with ones back facing down towards the deck, a bit hairy until one got used to doing it.

The next set of ratlines took one up to the crosstrees which were in line with the doublings of the top masts and to'gallant masts.

The next and final set of ratlines took one up to about the height of the Royal yard, when it was in its lowered position. To get onto the Royal yard when in its raised position, one shinned the last twelve or fourteen feet up the Royal backstay.

Monday & Tuesday 17 and 18/10/1938.

We turn to and are kept busy getting coal and stores aboard and all the small jobs one has to do in Port.

Wednesday 19/10/1933.

The last of the bagged wheat is discharged today, and we have a lively time chasing rats, and catch many, but quite a lot escape, including a very large albino. The ship is fumigated that same night and we collect many more dead rats the next day.

We have taken on 1,800 tons of ballast which consisted of clinker, ash and burnt refuse from the Glasgow Corporation incinerator.

Thursday 20/10/1938.

We move out of the berth in Princes dock (now sadly filled in this past several years) and go into Govan dry dock for the ships bottom to be cleaned and painted. In the next berth is Clan Lines 'CLAN MACARTHUR'.

Our Scottish passenger, joins us complete with several cases of whisky.

Olivebank in Govan dry dock 1938.

Saturday 22/10/1938.

This day we sign articles. The tugs 'CHIEFTAIN' and 'WARRIOR' arrive to take us from the dry dock and down river to Tail-of-the-Bank where we anchor.

The Clyde in those days was a busy water-way and we appeared to arouse much interest on our journey down river. We received rousing cheers and a few blasts of ships sirens as we passed ships moored at the various river side quays, and of course had a fine view of the 'QUEEN ELIZABETH' which was being built at John Browns Clyde Bank.

That evening we had a sing-song accompanied by Geoff's ukelele and donkey man's accordion. Alfred Holt's 'NESTOR' is anchored close by. She is a large ship indeed.

Monday 24/10/1938.

All hands today are busy bending sails, a hard and exacting job getting the sails out of the locker and carrying them to the foot of whichever mast they are to be sent up, and then made fast to a gantline (a tackle was used for the heavier sails) set the line to a capstan and then tramp, tramp away until you have got that sail hauled up to the required position, and then up aloft hauling the ear-rings out to the yard arm and make fast. Make the head of the sail fast, to the jackstay with rovings, make fast clew lines, bunt lines, sheets and leech lines, then down to the deck once more for a repeat performance until the sails on that mast were all bent.

Then we moved on to the next mast and did a repeat performance.

These sails were all fairly heavy, especially as this was all good strong heavy weather canvas which by the grace of God would withstand the stress of the winter North Atlantic gales.

The mainsail was obviously the heaviest of all the sails, in area about the size of a tennis court. Its bolt ropes were made of 1/2inch or 7/8ths of an inch diameter wire so, complete with its hardware of thimbles, spectacle plates, shackles and cringles, it would probably weigh around a ton.

Tuesday 25/10/1938.

Today we complete bending sail, no doubt to every ones joy as that certainly was some task and much 'breeches arse' steam has been used up in our efforts.

Wednesday and Thursday 26+27/10/1938.

We spend two days now down in the hold trimming ballast and laying dunnage over it, which is then lashed down in the hopes of containing both dunnage and ballast.

Friday 28/10/1938.

The tug 'CHIEFTAIN' arrives and we tramp the big capstan and break the anchor out. The tug blackens us and everything else with her black smoke and it was black and plenty of it. She takes us down to the open sea and meanwhile we are busy getting some sail on to 'OLIVEBANK'.

Off Arran Isle we slip the towline, the tug blows us a fond farewell on her whistle and we are on our way and on our own.

We get all sail set and then all hands are called aft and the Mates pick the watches. I am in the Starboard Watch.

We sail steadily down the Irish Sea course South half West and all night we see many lighthouses flashing on both the Scottish and Irish coasts.

Saturday 29/I0/1938.

The wind freshens up this afternoon and we get 3 blasts on the Mate's whistle calling out all hands, we take in Royals and courses, the wind shifts and we put her on the other tack and reset the courses. The wind by now is coming away stronger and blowing half a gale, and we can't get her through the St Georges Channel.

The wind is strengthening now and is a dead noser, and the old man decided to bring her about and run Northwards up the Irish Sea. We are now heeling well over and making about 14 knots (which is probably the most we made during all the voyage). We seemed to hurtle past the Calf of Man.

Presently we start to take in sail and run in towards Donaghadee (near Belfast Lough) and anchor about 2130 hrs. We then have a few hours real graft up aloft securing and stowing the remainder of the sails which were hanging in the buntlines, finally finishing this task at 0230 Sunday.

Sunday 30/10/I939.

We are now riding at anchor waiting for a fair wind.

Monday 31/10/1938.

We spend all day in the hold securing shifting boards over the ballast.

Tuesday 1/11/1938.

All of the starboard watch go aloft making fast some of the sails which have blown loose from the gaskets.

There is much wind and very squally but coming from the wrong direction.

We get caught aloft in a downpour of rain and hail and get drenched.

The wind freshens during the night and 'OLIVEBANK' starts to drag her anchor, so port watch are called out to let go the second anchor.

Wednesday 2/11/1938.

We are working on the ballast again today and then we heave up the port anchor, a long laborious task. We see a lot of shipping whilst laid here and can see very clearly the coasts of Scotland and the Isle of Man.

Thursday 3/11/1938.

Today we start to clear out the bilges where the ballast allows and get out a lot of grain, wet and sprouting and some just rotten. It gives off a 'lovely aroma' especially when mixed with dead rat. We let go the port anchor again at Midnight. A local fishing boat today very kindly brought us out some newspapers.

Friday 4/11/1938.

Today we start to 'soogey' down the paintwork with soda water, sand and canvas and at night we start to try to learn a little bit of each other's language. Some of the boys are writing down the words of some of their national and popular songs to while away the time.

Much disturbance at dinner time today as everyone is cursing the cook and the food. It seems the cat got into the galley and did something it shouldn't have. The poor old cook was so infuriated that his galley had been soiled that he killed the poor cat and now the crew say they will throw him overboard if he touches the kitten.

All the hands with the exception of Geoff Robertshaw and Per Finneman have now had all the hair shaved off their heads and are also trying to grow beards.

Tonight we have a sing song, the music again supplied by donkey man and Geoff also Unto Kanerva known now as 'the bull', because of his powerful build and short thick neck, was very good on the Tommy Talker. (Tommy Talkers are now called Kazoo's I believe.) The Lambeth Walk is very popular at the moment.

Tom Simpson at the helm of Miss Dorothy.

Sunday 6/11/1938.

The same fishing vessel came out again this afternoon with a party of 12 on board and once again kindly brought us more newspapers. All the party came aboard and had a good look round the ship and appeared to be very interested. On departing they took our mail for posting.

We had this day, a very large school of dolphins about 30 or 40 of them swimming and diving around the ship, a fine sight to behold. Today Tor Sontag gave me my first lesson in splicing wire, showing me how to do an eye splice. I must get in much practice as the splicing of wire and rope is an essential part of a seaman's job.

Monday 7/11/1938.

We wash down decks this morning which is routine and then once more into the hold we go to do another spot of bilge cleaning. The fishing vessel comes alongside for the last time, once again bringing out newspapers and cigarettes.

I believe the boat was owned by a fisherman named Skipper Tom Simpson and owing to stupidity on my part I forget the name of the vessel and regretfully I never got back to Donaghadee again or I would surely have looked up these very kind people.

Jack and his brother Skipper Tom Simpson on Miss Dorothy

Since writing this account I am very happy to say that with the kind co-operation of Captain Robert Hughes who is currently Harbour Master at Donaghadee (Oct 1983), I am now once more in touch with Skipper Tom Simpson who was Skipper and part owner of the fishing vessel "Miss Dorothy" B.350. This vessel was crewed by Tom, (facing camera) his father and brother Jack (facing away) and as stated they paid us several visits and were kindness itself bringing out cigarettes and newspapers and taking mail in for posting with, I feel, a considerable expense to themselves, as we crew members would for the most part be broke by this time, having spent our last few coppers around the dockside bars of Govan the night before we sailed.

Tom Simpson has sent me three very good photos to add to my collection, two of which he himself appears on, also a very fine one of 'OLIVEBANK' at anchor off Donaghadee.

Editors note. I have been unable to find these photographs mentioned by Len amongst his memorabilia but Tom's son 'Walker' has kindly sent me the photographs included in the text.

Tuesday 8/11/1938.

We weigh anchor today and there is a favourable wind to commence a run down the Irish Sea once again but by dusk the wind has once more hauled round and so the old man decides to bring 'OLIVEBANK' round and sail Northwards and this time we get out through the North Channel and out into the Atlantic. The wind comes away very strong during the night.

Wednesday 9/11/1938.

Today is very hectic as we shorten sail until we are under storm canvas and are now under lower top sails and one head sail. Several of us are first trippers and this is our first experience of really having to jump to it and get out onto the yards and get the sails secured into their gaskets. We have plenty of 'Pulley Haul' now and all of the, 'Armstrong patent' variety as we now do not have any steam to help us. All seemed to be utter confusion for a while (but no doubt only in the minds of those of us who were first trippers) as presently everything was snugged down, and each and every line was belayed and coiled down in its appropriate place, this being routine procedure after any manoeuvre of the sails, as every line and rope had its own appointed place, belayed either to the belaying pins on the fife rail around the mast or to the pins set in the pin-rail running fore and aft on the inboard side of the bulwarks. As there was a place for everything and everything in its place one soon learned to grab the correct line even on the blackest of black nights (but God help anybody who was caught making fast the wrong line to the wrong pin, they would most likely get a boot up the backside from Ragnar, as

44

I once did, or a hell of a bawling out should the 2nd Mate catch them). Broadly speaking the lines for the lower sails would be set onto the most forward of the pins and the higher the sail on the mast, the further aft the lines for that sail would be made fast.

Every line was belayed and coiled down

Thursday 10/11/1938 and Friday 11/11/1938.

Very strong wind and big sea running and we are heading out into the North Atlantic and close hauled on the port tack, heading about W.N.W. going crab fashion and making a fair amount of leeway. Theoretically some of these big square riggers can sail within four and a half to five points of the winds eye when close hauled, with the yards braced right up onto the backstays but they also make quite a lot of leeway.

Saturday 12/11/1938.

Wind eases away a bit and we set the upper topsails, staysails, fore sail and mainsail and presently the wind hauls round a few points and we change course and start to make some Southing. Towards night the wind drops away quite a bit and we get on more sail which does not last very long as the wind soon freshens again and once more we shorten sail.

The wind keeps shifting a few points this way and that and we spend a lively time all through Saturday night and Sunday morning taking and making sail and bracing up the yards to try and keep her on a steady course. Much kicking and cursing by the crew at all this toil, but it has to be done.

Sunday 13/11/1938.

The wind shifts again and becomes unfavourable and we are once again on a westerly course. Tacking and making sail is now the order of the day and night and this continues for the next few days. The wind velocity seems to vary quite a lot, but we have a heavy sea running all the time and it is fairly cold with some rain and sleet.

During this period Blomquist and self are sent up to take the main Royal (this being my first experience of furling a Royal sail in the dark and in atrocious weather to boot). Up we go onto that Royal yard about 170ft above deck level, the masts were describing a great arc in the sky, it was bitterly cold and the canvas stiff and wet. The sail was ballooning out as at least one of the buntlines had carried away. We were not making any headway gathering that kicking canvas and eventually Blomquist being the fine and experienced sailor that he was grabbed the wire lift which held the Royal yard, heaved himself up and walked and trampled on that ballooning canvas until I could gather it sufficiently to pass some gaskets round it and snug it down. Far below one could make out through the darkness the white of the heavily breaking seas and it was a most exhilarating experience and one which I shall never forget. From that night onwards, heights have never caused me any apprehension whatever, though one must always be mindful of the dangers when working aloft and try not to be foolhardy.

After several days of beating to Westward the wind eases a touch and comes round a few points and we are able to start the run southwards.

Now that the weather has eased away and we are running a steady course, we first trippers commence to take our trick at the wheel. No instruction was given and it was a bit awe inspiring to go up to that holy of holies the poop and take over the wheel for the first time.

Sad to say I was soon in disgrace as I went two points off course to Port

46

and in my haste to remedy this I gave her too much helm in the opposite direction (instead of trying to bring her back on course steadily), with the result, that I soon had her two and a half points off course to starboard. Up charged the 2nd Mate taking a quick look at the steering compass and blew a blast on his whistle calling up a relief helmsman and I was then, very ignominiously relieved of my first trick on the wheel and was the recipient of some hard looks and even harder words from the 2nd Mate.

I don't think the lad who had to relieve me was too pleased either as it was night time. The time he would have been able to stay in the bunk had he so wished and would only have had to turn out for sail handling or the like, so in fact my stupidity was his loss, but he took it all in good part and happily we remained good shipmates.

When daylight came the 2nd Mate, as was customary, walked up the deck and checked the sails of each mast in turn, to see if any of the rope yarn stoppers which held the bunt-lines slack had parted during the night - several had! It was usual to send up the first trippers to perform this task of overhauling the buntlines.

One went aloft armed with rope yarn strands, caught hold of the buntline and hauled it up a little, thus giving a bit more slack on the buntline between the block on the mast through which it was rove and the foot of the sail to which it was made fast, using a rope yarn. The buntline was then stopped off just below the block, thus allowing the sail to draw more fully and also to save a certain amount of chafe on the sail. One hard tug on the buntline was usually enough to break the rope yarn when the sail was to be clewed up.

On reaching the deck after having accomplished the task on the mizzen Royal, I was confronted by the 2nd Mate who appeared to have a wicked glint in his eye and I was sent up to the Main Royal to perform another buntline overhaul. This was most unusual as each man would normally only be required to perform this duty on any one mast as a matter of early morning routine.

On reaching the deck once more I was again confronted by Mr Anderson with what I was now sure was a wicked glint in his eyes and was detailed off to clean out the pig pen. I somehow got the message that at this time I did not qualify for the title of 2nd Mates blue eyed boy.

We are by now heading in a southerly direction and making steady progress and see many vessels as we cross over several shipping lanes leading to and from the Irish Sea, Bristol and English Channels.

Days and dates will now not follow consecutively, but where given will be correct in relation to the event narrated.

We are now making steady progress in a southerly direction the temperature is now increasing day by day and we are having too much sail drill. Most of us spend much of our time chipping rust and red leading down in the tween decks.

I have now learned to steer, having taken some instruction from Blomquist and Finneman (in my free time) and though the 2nd Mate keeps a careful eye on the compass, I seem now to be fairly satisfactory, but I am still getting more than a fair share of pig pen duties (which I happen to like), as the fact is that one can have a few crafty drags on a cigarette whilst in the pig pen, as long as one keeps a weather eye open watching through the port hole for the approach of the enemy.

I happen to have two uncles at home who have small farms and both keep pigs, so really this is no punishment to me at all, but I have no intention of taking the second mate into my confidence regarding this little matter.

I have now learned to steer.

We sight a steamer in 30°N and signal her by morse lamp, this is the first vessel we have seen for several days as we are now well away from the normal shipping lanes. We have now picked up the North East Trade Wind and 'OLIVEBANK' is making steady headway.

The weather is getting much warmer but not unpleasantly hot, though foolishly I allowed my shoulders and back to get too much sun and they are rather badly blistered.

We experience several heavy rain squalls at this time and spread some of the smaller sails which we get out of the sail locker and thus catch a lot of good fresh water for our daily use and top up most of our storage tanks. Those of us who are not on watch emerge from our fo'c'sles in the 'altogether' armed with a bar of soap and enjoy a real good shower.

We have made good time and we are now down in the tropics south of Latitude 23° N. This is truly flying fish weather and really beautiful. Most every morning at daybreak we pick up flying fish which have landed aboard during the night. They are mostly around eight inches to a foot in length, but do not have too much flesh on them, so we do not eat them. Some of the crew gut and dry them, mount them on boards and give them a coat of varnish and they make nice trophies.

Whilst we have been running with the trade wind we have not had a lot of sail drill, as the wind blows fairly constantly from the same direction, and sometimes all we have had to do has been to give a good swing up on the braces, about once and sometimes twice a watch.

Consequently many of the watch have gone on day work and much ships maintenance is now being carried out.   The more experienced men are now re-serving and re-seizing the standing rigging, while the ordinary seamen and deckboys are still busy painting in the tween decks. Some of us have stinging eyes at the end of the watch caused by fumes thrown out by the paint when it is applied to the hot metal of hull plates and deck heads.

We get a bottle of highly concentrated lime juice per six men per week while in the tropics and when diluted makes a very refreshing drink and helps to keep away scurvy.

Friday 2/12/1938.

We are now in the doldrums belt and making very little headway, a lot of the time the sails are just hanging limp from the yards, slatting and chafing, caused by the movement of the vessel as she rolls in the oily swell. The old man and mates are kept very alert watching for each catspaw of wind as it ruffles the surface of the water in the near distance, then it's all the watch and daymen to the braces, to be ready for trimming the yards to try and catch what little breeze comes our way.

Sunday 4/12/1938.

We cross the line this forenoon and Father Neptune and all his retinue emerge from the night heads with much pomp and circumstance, bowing and scraping and the blowing of a trumpet.

Crossing the Line

We five poor unfortunate first trippers who were initiated - Sam Johansson, Borge Kulberg, Albin Bjorkman, Gunnar Lindross and Len

Townend are arrested, made to strip completely and are then chained together and led chain gang wise up on to the poop.

Then still shackled we circumnavigate the entire length and breadth of the decks. Finally we are unshackled at No.3 hatch and are then subjected to the usual shaving and ducking ceremony. We are examined by Neptune's Doctor who prescribes medicine? I don't really know what it contained but it appeared to have a fair amount of curry in it and tasted like soup made out of boiled sweaty sea boot stockings and a few drops of paraffin. "Bloody awful", is the kindest comment I could make about it.

I was stripped, chained and led around the deck

The ceremony drew to a bawdy close when Neptune's artists got to work with their brushes. Tar, red lead, paint and black grease were all being very liberally used and spread around in places on the anatomy both mentionable and unmentionable. However, a good time was had by all. (I think??)

Tuesday 6/12/1938.

Today we have a holiday as we celebrate 'Freedom Day', when Finland cast off the Russian yoke in 1919.

Many of the crew are now making models of 'OLIVEBANK' a popular size seems to be a wooden hull about ten inches in length, complete with all deck houses, etc. Masts are made of wood, yards made out of strands of seizing wire and billowing sails out of shaped sections cut from tooth paste tubes. Everything is painted in authentic ships paint and mounted in a glass case sailing on a sea of putty with a bit of painted landscape and a lighthouse for a backdrop.

Per Finneman started to make a very fine model of 'OLIVEBANK' last trip. It is about three feet in length and a picture to look at. The yards all move freely and it would appear that all the blocks and tackles work also, truly a very fine effort and one of which he can be proud indeed.

Wednesday 7/12/1938.

We start the heavy graft again today, as we are bringing the lighter sails on deck, mending where necessary prior to changing them, as now we are about to pick up the South East Trade Wind. Hopefully we shall be in more moderate weather and not require the heavier sails used in the North Atlantic.

We now have a fairly strong breeze and so far we have only changed the three course sails, spanker and gaff topsail and stay sails.

There is great excitement this afternoon as while we are aloft we sight a sail. We think it may be 'PENANG' homeward bound. ('PENANG' had suffered a broken main top mast on the way down to the Horn and spent about 2 months getting repaired in New Zealand and did not arrive in the U.K. until mid December 1938 taking 210 days from the Spencer Gulf).

Timberman (Chippy, Kaiku Luotonen) is now in his element, tearing up old and worn deck planking. I am detailed off to help him with this job and also I have the job of chipping the scale off the metal deck underneath the planking and giving the scaled portions a liberal coating of red lead, after which Chippy relays new planking.

Chippy is a great character and speaks only Finnish, so between us we conjure up many new words and oddly enough we seem to be able to converse in our own odd fashion.

Thursday 8/12/1938.

The sailing vessel is much nearer this morning and is dead ahead of us and travelling South. We now think it is either 'LAWHILL' or 'MOSHULU' and not 'PENANG' but she draws steadily away and is out of sight by noon. We are now well south of the line and for the next 8 days or so we experience doldrums weather with the usual puffs of wind and heavy tropical rain squalls.

Plenty of drill bracing round the yards, this way and that, to try and catch every last puff, and also once more we are able to catch some good fresh water to top up the water tanks.

Plenty of drill bracing round the yards

Arne Laakso and self go up to make fast the fore royal during the night in a rain squall and get soaked to the skin.

53

We have had 2 albatross with us for a few days now, they soar around us in the lightest of airs and settle on the water close by when the ship is becalmed and we feed them scraps of bread, etc.

We are now about latitude 20 degrees south and once more sight a sailing vessel many miles astern of us, but we soon forge ahead and lose her.

Saturday 17/12/1938.

We have picked up the South East Trade Wind now. It is good and steady and 'OLIVEBANK' is making good headway. We are steering by the wind at the moment, the lower yards being braced hard up to the backstays to get the full benefit of the wind, whilst the royal yards are not braced up as sharply and one has just to keep the leech of the mizzen royal fluttering gently to keep the ship heading as near as possible to the required course.

Lower yards braced hard up to the backstays

I am getting much practice at the wheel now, two and a half hours today all of it under the watchful eye of the old man and he and I have the Poop to ourselves as the Mates are down on deck supervising, once again, the changing of the sails from the tropical rags back to heavy canvas for the run South.

I much prefer to steer by the wind than by compass course, much more interesting, and with the odd pleasant word of guidance from Capt. Granith.

The day men have now been put back into the watches as from now on we can expect steadier and stronger winds as we head further south.

The rats must be breeding steadily as they have now emerged on to the deck at night. We caught one last night under one of the capstans and gave it to the cat and she made short work of it while the rats are making short work of our remaining potatoes. They gnaw bits out of them and soil and defile the remainder.

We appear to have read most of our books by now so the usual recreations are model making, playing with the cat, listening to our musicians or just sitting around having multi-lingual swearing sessions.

Sunday 18/12/1938.

We are well down into the South Atlantic and several hundred miles east of the mainland of South Africa and we have a large pod of whales all around us and some of them are very close to the ship. They are heading southwards, no doubt migrating to the summer feeding grounds of the Antarctic. There must be several thousands of them as they are still around us after nightfall, and the noise as they exhale is somewhat eerie. Also present are many small black and white birds called stormy petrels or Mother Carey's chickens.

Tuesday 20/12/1938.

Today we have many albatross soaring gracefully around, big beautiful birds and a joy to watch as they glide and swoop through the air in what would appear to be effortless and nearly perpetual flight, with hardly a flap of their wings.

Chippy managed to catch one with his trap, which consists of a piece of board about ten inches by three inches which acts as a float. Attached to one end of the float is a piece of wire in the shape of a V and into the apex of this V is fastened a piece of salt pork for bait. Once, the bird gets its beak around the bait and the wire, one simply takes the strain and hauls the bird and float up on deck.

The albatross has a big curve, in the end of its beak so that when it gets hold of the wire and the bait it really hooks itself on. Probably once the strain is taken on the line it is unable to let go of its own free will.

On the other hand it may be like the monkeys which are caught in some areas, simple by putting nuts and fruit etc into some object which has holes drilled into it, which allows room for the monkey to put its paws through to grab the bait but is not large enough for the withdrawal of paw and bait.

Albatross are fine big birds and it is nothing unusual for them to measure 8 to 10 feet wing tip to wing tip. They seem to have difficulty walking and are somewhat clumsy of movement on deck but they have a very sharp beak and could probably inflict severe damage with it.

We catch an albatross

We took several photos of the big bird and put the kitten on its back which was not enjoyed by either of them. The albatross snapped its beak menacingly causing the kitten to beat a hasty retreat. We lowered the albatross down to the water and away it swam.

Work is still going ahead on all the standing rigging, re-serving and re-seizing the stays and then setting them up tight and finally coating the threads on the bottle screws with tallow and white lead, worming them with spun yarn and last of all tightly stitching canvas jackets over most all of the bottle screws to keep out the water and thus keeping them rust free. The crew, seem to think that all this attention to the standing rigging is a sure indication that we shall go home by way of Cape Horn.

Wednesday 21/12/1938.

We have experienced variable winds, regarding both velocity and direction this past few days, but today we have got the westerlies and it is now blowing fairly hard with a big following sea, also heavy rain squalls and a lot of mist and it is now feeling much colder. We take in all royals, two outer head sails and spanker gaff topsail.

The lookout men have, been told to keep an extra good look out and to keep the fog horn going during the squalls and mist patches. Sadly the old fog horn has seen better days (or else the mist and wet weather has affected its chest) for even with maximum effort winding the handle we seem only to get a wheeze and a few splutters and never anything that resembles the full throated roar. We are steering E NE. half E.

Saturday 24/12/1938. Christmas Eve.

We have had a steady wind and mixed weather since Wednesday. The wind remains steady and is coming from directly aft and a fairly big following sea is running. Under these conditions great care must be taken when at the wheel, for she will soon go off course and start to roll badly if the helmsman fails to keep her on a steady course.

It is still getting colder and there are many stormy petrels flitting about and several albatross air-borne around the ship.

Despite the wind and temperature it is a beautiful day with blue sky and much sunshine.

Noon position. Course N.E. by E.half E. Pos: 41° 48'S 5° 13'W.

57

All hands are called aft and the Captain gives us each our Motbok (notebook) which contains extracts from Finnish Maritime Law.

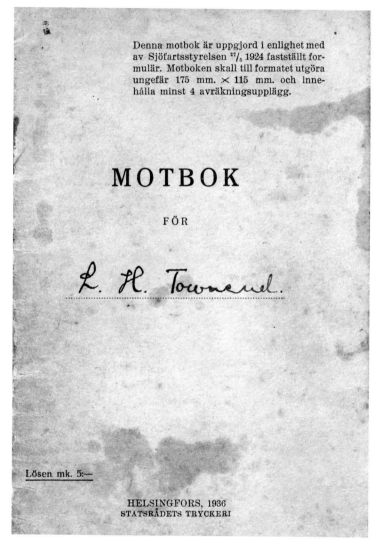

Denna motbok är uppgjord i enlighet med av Sjöfartsstyrelsen ²⁷/₅ 1924 fastställt formulär. Motboken skall till formatet utgöra ungefär 175 mm. × 115 mm. och innehålla minst 4 avräkningsupplägg.

MOTBOK

FÖR

L. H. Townend.

Lösen mk. 5:—

HELSINGFORS, 1936
STATSRÅDETS TRYCKERI

There are also several entries, i.e. name of seaman, home address, name of vessel, and port of Registry, Rank or rating, pay per month, port and date of signing on, Master's signature. Also there are spaces for the Port at which the seaman is paid off and on what date and once again the Masters signature.

This section of the book is giving roughly the same details as the several entries which would be made in a British Seamans continuous certificate of discharge book and I should imagine with the same purpose.

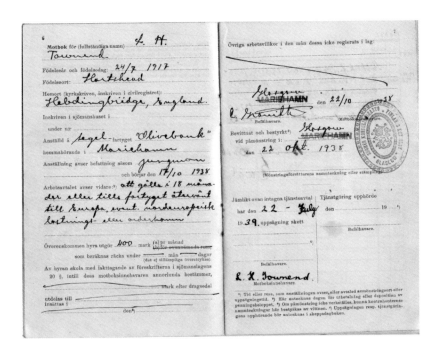

Additionally the Motbok contains several pages for debit and credit and on these pages are kept the accounts of purchases from slop chest, subs in port etc, etc. In brief it is a discharge book, an account of wages and a copy of the relevant articles of agreement.

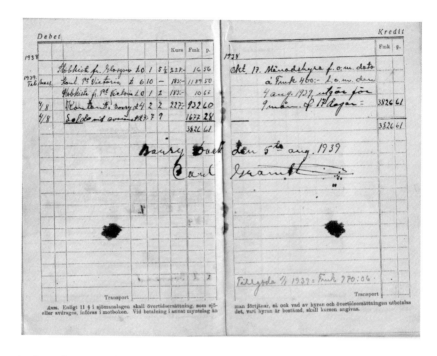

I signed on as Jungman (deck-boy). Wage in Finn marks 400 per month on a voyage which may be of 18 months duration or else until the vessel arrives back to a European port of discharge or North European loading port or order haven.

After we have received our Motboks, we next draw lots from the Mates cap and we each receive a Christmas present which has the corresponding number attached to it. I am glad to receive a pair of hand knitted wool mitts and a Christmas card from the sender. Aina Karlson of Esplanadagaten, Mariehamn. Fortyfour years on in 1983 I still have the card, but not the mitts. They saved my hands quite a lot from the cold as we got further south and were much worn by me.

Tonight we all have a good and happy Christmas sing song. During this night we observe many shooting stars up in the sky, which to us simple sailormen is a sure sign that the birthday of our Lord is being heralded in.

Sunday 25/12/1935. Christmas Day.

I was lookout from 3am to 4am and a beautiful dawn broke this morning and we had good weather with a steady following wind. By early afternoon the mist came down and it became very cold, and a lookout was posted on the fo'c'sle head and given instruction to keep a sharp look out for ice.

Today is a holiday and only normal working of the ship is taking place. The Mate has put on his best uniform for Christmas and is strutting up and down the deck looking very pleased with himself.

Noon position. 40° O'S 1° O'W. Course N.E. threequarters E.

We are bowling along on the port tack, carrying all sail and making 13 knots. A large black and white fish is swimming about just ahead of the forefoot - we think it is an Albacore. One of the tunny family.

Towards night fall the wind freshens a bit and the Old Man comes on deck and gives orders to take in the Royals, Spanker and gaff topsail. She is very heavy to steer tonight, as the wheel is kicking and bucking and making it very hard work. Rolf Forsman the cook has made us a lovely Christmas cake.

Monday 26/12/1938. Boxing Day.

Today is also a holiday but we get plenty of work bracing up, first one way, and then the other as the wind is not constant but is shifting about a few points, though still coming in from astern. We take in all stay sails as they are of little use at the moment.

As it is summer time down in the Southern hemisphere dawn breaks around 3.30am and we have daylight until 9 pm. It is very wet and cold through the early morning, but brightens up as the day goes on. The wind steadies and becomes constant once more, but with a heavy sea running up from astern so once again we are making good headway.

Noon position. 42° 40'S. 7° 27' E. (This is the best days run noon to noon since we left U.K.).

Tuesday 27/12/1938.

We are now down in the roaring forties, running our eastern down.

Running our Eastern down. Photo Len Townend.

The wind down here surely does roar and plays deep bass tunes in the rigging, easing away for a few minutes and then once more comes the loud roaring noise.

When one first experiences this noise it is quite deafening, but one soon becomes accustomed to it.

I have been much further south down into the howling or raging fifties and screaming sixties in power driven vessels but the effect is not the same or the noise so loud as it is with the wind playing the harp strings of a windjammers rigging.

We have a very strong following wind and very heavy sea running and the ship is rolling very heavily. The day is bright and clear but there are frequent rain and hail squalls and it is very cold on deck. We are now charging through the water making 12 knots and getting a little water on deck from time to time just to make it a bit more interesting. The Royals, staysails and spanker are still fast in their gaskets but we are tearing away. There are two men at the wheel all morning as she was too heavy for one man to manage.

Many of us are now getting deep cuts in the palms of our hands, this is caused by the wet and cold and the extra force one has to use to try and hold that kicking and bucking steering wheel.

Noon position. 42°0'S 13° 37'E. Steering course ESE.half E.

The pig pen duties have now returned to a strict rota with each 'first tripper' taking his turn. I don't know if I am now out of the dog house or if the 2nd Mate has found out that I like pigs.

Today I spend all my free time trying to teach Kangas a bit of basic English, not an easy job, as he only speaks Finnish.

Wednesday 28/12/19.

A very cold day again today with a strong, steady wind and fairly heavy sea running and much hail and sleet. Port watch have the job of setting Royals. Usual routine duties for the 1st trippers, cleaning pig pen, lavatories and getting coal for the galley and of course taking ones turn as 'Peggy', that is washing the crews eating utensils and cleaning out both fo'c'sles, followed by another stint of sorting and de-sprouting our few remaining potatoes.

Senior crew members are busy renewing some of the running gear, such as buntlines, clewlines etc. as this wind and weather soon take their toll on old worn cordage. Noon Position. 42°0'S 19°51'E steering course E.

'OLIVEBANK' is now about 420 miles south of Cape Agullas which is the southern most tip of the African continent.

Thursday 29/12/1938.

The wind eased away during the night so we are not making much speed. It is much warmer this morning but there is rain again in the afternoon.

The Port, watch set all stay sails and have had a strenuous hour or so tightening up the braces.

I have been helping Chippy again relaying more deck planking. He caught another albatross at dinner time about 9ft wing span. We put it back over the side and it swam back to join its mates.

Much bracing all afternoon as the wind is shifting, about.

Noon position. 42° 35'S 24° 37'E

Friday. 30/12/1938.

There is very little wind all day and it is very cold and very wet. We spend nearly all watch at the bloody braces, trying to catch every puff of wind.

The only things that are making any progress are the "sodding" sea cracks on our hands, these bastards are progressing alright, but in the wrong direction, as they are getting longer and deeper.

Towards night the wind freshens and the starboard watch take in the royals Arne Laasko and self taking the fore royal.

Saturday 31/12/1938.

Very nice weather today as the rain has stopped but it is very cool. We are now in the Southern Indian Ocean and have a steady breeze so we set the royals again this morning, steering by the wind with course about East by South. As night falls the winds become more variable and we in the 1900 to 2400hrs watch have to provide much 'breeches arse' steam as we are kept at it constantly trimming the yards.

I had the last wheel and had the honour of steering the ship into the New Year. At midnight I struck 24 bells as I had been instructed to do by some of the older hands, this in turn being repeated by the lookout with the big bell on the foc'sle head. The 2nd Mate was most displeased and gave the pair of us "Hell" for making such a din. Seemingly we should have only struck 16 bells to herald in the New Year.

Ah well! Perhaps sex repression was beginning to wear on the nerves of some of us a bit, that's what we shall have to put it down to.

The milk ration has been improved upon, as we now get one tin of condensed milk per man per week which is a big improvement on 2 tins per week per 6 men. It is now up to each of us to mark our tin and see to it that immediately after use we plug up the 2 holes we have pierced in the lid to stop the cockroaches, of which we have an abundance, from getting into the milk and drowning.

Noon Position. 41°50'S. 31°24'E.

Sunday January 1st 1939. New Years Day.

I was policeman 4am to 5am this morning and for some reason or other I forgot to call the cook at 4.30am, so the 2nd Mates coffee was not ready sharp at 5.30am. Once more he gives me "Hell" and it didn't do his blood pressure any good either, for he went the colour of a black-red beetroot. What with the midnight incident of the bells and now this, I feel I shall be overhauling buntlines and swilling out the lavatories for the remainder of the voyage. The pig job would be alright but I fancy he now knows that I prefer pigs to certain individuals.

We are under full sail and are now making better speed as we have now set all try sails and the wind has freshened a bit. The day is beautiful and on our free watch we sit on No 3 hatch playing cards or reading. By 6pm the wind falls away and shifts round so we now have the wind from right astern, so we brace the yards and take in all stay sails. Course E.quarter South.

Monday 2/1/1939.

Once more it is a lovely day with only a light breeze and a very calm sea. Several albatross are overhead and one or two black birds very much like crows are flying around,

The 3rd Mate is very upset as he cannot find his constant companion the cat. He has been looking for it all over the ship for he loves the little animal dearly and spends most of his free time playing with it. Happily it is eventually found safe and sound down in the hold. He is once more a happy man and bursts into his favourite Pola Negri song (in Finnish of course) the first few lines being as follows:

MINTJN SYDAMENI KAIPAA, TUOTA ONNEN AIKAA, MI HETKEN KESTI, KERRAN NUOTUUDESSAIN.

After all the years that have elapsed between 1938/39 and the attempted writing of this log in the summer of 1983 I can still recall the tune.

Noon position. 42°18'S. 36°38'E.

Tuesday 3/1/1939.

The wind has disappeared and we are becalmed all day and the water is very clear. We experience a beautiful sunrise and sunset with an unbroken stretch of 16 hrs of sunshine.

Towards evening we have about 20 albatross swimming around us like big ducks and making a lot of noise as they fight for the scraps of food we throw them. We catch two big ones but presently put them back in the water without causing them any harm.

The sails are slatting and banging in the rigging and we have clewed up the courses to save unnecessary wear and tear on them.

We had a good laugh tonight as big Unto Kanerva (the bull) has been giving equally large Tor Sontag rides round the capstan. Sontag sitting in the centre of the capstan while Kanerva runs round and round pushing the capstan bar.

Course East   but little headway today.

Wednesday 4/1/1939.

No wind today, the ship has not even got steerage way and there is an oily swell. There are about 5 albatross round us and we try to catch some in our free watch but no luck.

Sailmaker Niilo Kangas (left) and Julius Henriksson

Ships maintenance includes Chippy carrying on with relaying of deck planks, sailmaker Niilo Kangas and Julius Henriksson have sails stretched out on deck drying and are both busy with palms, needles and twine. Donkeyman, Vaino Makinen is busy de-scaling his boiler and overhauling the winches ready for use in the Spencer Gulf. The rest of us are overhauling the running gear and the less intelligent of us, in which category I got full marks, are chipping rust and red leading. A breath of wind tonight and we sheet home the foresail.

Noon position. 42° 32'South 39°0'E.

Thursday 5/1/1939.

We are becalmed once again this morning and rolling a bit in the oily swell. Presently we get a light breeze and start to run about 4 knots. We tack twice today and are steering by the wind.

Friday 6/1/1939.

Today is a holiday 'Epiphany'. Very wet and foggy and we have had to have a fo'c'sle head lookout posted all day. The wind is a little stronger than yesterday and we are still by-the-wind, heading East half South.

For today's natural history lesson we have shoals of small fish passing underneath the ship, 7 or 8 albacores come playing under the bows for a considerable time, they have very conspicuous black and white markings and are as graceful in the water as the albatross in the air currents. We also see several cape pigeons and a black molly hawk.

There was much hilarity in our fo'c'sle tonight as Bjorkman, Lindross, Kulberg and Halpo Alanen endeavoured to do a Swedish crossword, aided by Geoff and myself who threw in the odd inane remark. Plenty of music all night as we have to keep the fog horn wheezing away.

Steering East threequarters North.

Saturday 7/1/1939.

A nice clear forenoon with a freshening breeze and so we make rather better headway. Donkeyman gives us some musical relief this evening with several tunes on his accordion. One of his favourites and mine is a very catchy Scandinavian tune entitled 'Na skall vi opp, opp, opp'. (Now shall we go up, up, up.) it is a great favourite with all the crew.

Sunday 8/1/1939.

A fine dry morning, but as the day progresses the wind starts to blow much stronger and we have a very heavy following sea. The big whaleback affords the helmsman much shelter on these occasions and I for one appreciate it and the amount of cover it gives us from the sea, wind and rain. We run all day on the port tack, close hauled. Towards nightfall the wind really comes away and we have plenty of graft all watch as we shorten down to storm canvas, taking in royals, upper and lower top gallants, courses, spanker, gaff topsail, and some of the stay sails. Vessel making about 12 knots and she seems to be flying along.

Storm canvas set

Monday 9/1/1939.

It is blowing hells bells this morning with long spells of heavy rain and it is very cold indeed and a very big sea is running. Old "OLIVEBANK" is really running even under such shortened canvas and she is really making the spray fly high, much better here than serving on some rich gentlemans yacht. Several of my old school mates in Bridlington, crewed in yachts from time to time as Bridlington is the headquarters of The Royal Yorkshire Yacht Club.

By noon the wind falls away quite a bit and once again we spend nearly all watch getting canvas back on her and by the change of the watch she is carrying everything except royals, spanker, gaff topsail and some of the stay sails.

The wheel has been easy enough and for some reason has done little kicking this watch. We change course from East half North to ESE half E and brace round as the wind is once again coming up from astern.

Noon position. 43°4'S 51°35'E.

Friday 13/1/1939.

We have had a good wind since Monday and have covered much ground and were able to carry Royals nearly all week, but the wind strengthened and we took in the Royals again this afternoon.

This week as for some time past, we have had a lot of very cold rain and some fairly high seas and on deck one has had to wear oilskins much of the time and so now most of us have, along with the enlarged sea cracks on our hands due to a kicking wheel and much 'pulley haul', the added discomfort of salt water boils around our wrists. This is caused chiefly by the cuffs of our oilskins chafing against our wrists and is not peculiar or particular to sailing ship men. I have had them as a fisherman and on winter time runs across the Western Ocean but they are something one can quite well do without and it is surprising how one always seems to knock the tender parts when working aloft. The pain causes tears in the eyes and the issuing forth of much foul and obscene language

Saturday 14/1/1939.

The wind has eased a bit and we set royals. Still the same miserable, rain, but never mind we are well on our way now to sunny Australia, which is a cheering thought.

Apart from working the ship and every day routine jobs, we have 'soogyed' down all the outside white paintwork with soda water, sand and canvas to remove the rust stains. The paintwork looks much improved but the soda and the sand have not been in any way complimentary to sea cracks and boils, in fact it's made the bastards bigger, deeper and much more painful.

The other job of the week has been down in the hold lime washing out the sections of bilges that we had hitherto cleaned out, to sweeten them up ready for the grain cargo. Also we were rigging sweatboards around the heavier stanchions and wrapping the lighter stanchions down in the hold with strips of burlap so that our pending wheat cargo would not become affected by condensation.

There have been 2 men at the wheel for most of the last few days. Course has varied from East by North to East South East for all this period of time.

Noon position. 43°0' South. 78°34' E.

Sunday 15/1/1939.

A change of weather today, bright sunshine and much warmer, a lovely white capped blue sea. Wind variable and both watches have done a lot of sweating at the braces. The sunshine and the warmth both cheers and heartens we poor lost souls no end. The 2nd Mate saw me messing about with some bits of rope this afternoon and came across and showed me how to splice 4 strand manilla rope, which was very good of him. Perhaps the sunshine had cheered him up a bit too.

The average daily distance run for the last 6 days has been 270 miles per day and our furthest point south has been 43°58' south. We still have a few albatross and molly hawks with us. At night the sea sparkles and is very phosphorescent.

Thursday 19/1/1939.

We have had a steady but gentle wind since Sunday.

Noon position. 43°0' S. 100°4' E.

We have been busy almost all of the week down in the holds, preparing for the cargo. Lifting spare ceiling and limber boards, wherever the ballast allows this and coating the inside of the bottom plates, i.e. floor, frames and keelson with either lime or cement wash.

There was much excitement as we sight a sail about 5am and as we are only travelling slowly we heave to and wait for her coming up. She draws level about 3.30pm and proves to be the barque 'WINTERHUDE' 80 days out from Gothenburg. She comes quite close and exchanges messages, first by semaphore and then by speaking trumpet. She spoke to the same steamer as we did in the North Atlantic and also rounded the Cape of Good Hope the same day as us.

Winterhude from Olivebank 1939

When we have exchanged our greetings we brace up a bit and start to draw slowly ahead. 'OLIVEBANK' being the much larger vessel with four masts, 'WINTERHUDE' only having three masts and having a bald headed rig i.e. she carried only 5 square sails each on the fore and main masts and did not cross royal yards above the upper topgallants.

Friday 20/1/1939.

On the voyage out the fresh water pump leading from the domestic tank developed a fault and was out of order for some time, so during this period it was the job of 2 deck boys to get up the ration of drinking water for the saloon, galley and both fo'c'sles each morning. One boy to go down on the tank top in the tween decks, remove the inspection cover and use a bucket and rope to get out the water, which in turn was passed up to the other lad on deck who then distributed it to its appointed place.

The water had been slightly tainted for some time, but we just put this down to the fact that by now the water level would be well down and that as we had run through quite a lot of warm weather the water was stale and brackish.

On the morning of the 19/1/39 it was my turn to go into the tween decks and in the first bucketful I drew out of the tank was a decomposed rat, stinking to high heaven so this, of course, was the main reason for the water being a bit "off".

We all had strict instructions always to replace the inspection cover after we had got out the days water supply, (1) for safety reasons and, (2) to keep the water clean and vermin free. This order was not always carried out and on several occasions the cover had been left off over night hence the rat in the tank.

No one seemed to be any the worse for having drunk the water so we must all have had tough constitutions by this time.

Saturday 21/1/1939.

We are with 'WINTERHUDE' once more.

Captain Carl Granith in foreground 1939

There is little wind and a calm sea, so the main yards are braced around and the ship put in irons.

Our motor boat is put over the side, amidst much shouting from the Mates and Captain Granith, the 2nd Mate, Artur Blomquist and our Scottish passenger who we have christened Hong Kong because of his yellow hue set off for 'WINTERHUDE'. Unfortunately they experience some engine trouble en-route and have to row the rest of the way.

When they arrive back in the afternoon they bring with them Captain Holm a lady passenger and two children to visit 'OLIVEBANK'

The English boys in 'WINTERHUDE' have kindly sent us some books over, which will be much enjoyed by us.

When our boat returns to 'WINTERHUDE' with our visitors, this time manned by our Mate and 3rd Mate, we send some of our books over to the boys on 'WINTERHUDE'.

They got the motor running again, but on the journey back to 'OLIVEBANK' it peters out once more and the two Mates have to row. When they arrived back alongside us it was very obvious that a convivial atmosphere must have prevailed during the period of the visit, for both mates were starry eyed, as were the 2nd Mate and Blomquist when they had arrived back earlier.

As for our passenger who had remained over on 'WINTERHUDE' during all these comings and goings, he was glassy eyed and as full up as he could get and quite incapable, so we hauled him aboard in a sling. I must confess I half hoped the sling or the rope would carry away so that we could see if the salt water sobered him up a bit, but his luck held and we dumped him very unceremoniously on deck and left him there as we had other urgent matters to attend to.

We now had to get the motor boat aboard and this we did, urged on with much encouragement from the Mates and a lot of shouting and bawling as well. Whilst bringing the boat inboard something went wrong with the tackle and she fetched up with a bit of a bang on top of the deck house which caused some superficial damage to the structure. Happily nothing very serious and Chippy rectified matters during the next few days.

The revelry carried on into the evening at which time the Mate and Hong Kong (the passenger) who must have been disagreeing on some point or other emerged from the poop and the Mate then thumped him a couple of times. No damage done (not even to pride) as they were both so pissed by now that the blows were ineffectual and by next morning neither of them would have remembered anything about it.

Sunday 22/1/1939.

We are now gradually drawing away from 'WINTERHUDE' who is heading more easterly than us. 'OLIVEBANK' making about 4 knots and steering NE by E threequarters E.

Noon position. 42°45' South. 105°9' East.

75

Monday 23/1/1939 to Friday 27/1/1939.

We have a fairly constant and steady breeze during this time. Both fo'c'sles have been washed out with soogy and have been painted out, during which time we have all slept for four nights down in the tween decks, with the odd rat for company.

Rats we have a plentiful supply of and also cockroaches, but happily none of these other nasty bed companions, 'bed bugs'. Not once during the voyage did I encounter these filthy creatures which I feel says much indeed for the cleanliness of the crew, as on voyages through warm weather, the straw filling of the mattresses or donkey's breakfasts as we called them are just what they thrive on, along with the blood of humans. I have been in good clean ships with rubber mattresses and have from time to time been plagued with the filthy things. Often they used to come aboard with the 'clean' linen from the dubious laundries of the Middle East etc.

Once when I was bosun on M.V. 'HOUSTON CITY', out of Bideford (Sir Willam Reardon Smith, Shipowners, Cardiff), I must have not been too popular with one of the crew for he emptied a match box full of the creatures under my pillow. He suffered for his misdeeds in more ways than one, over a long period of time, in much worse ways than cleaning out the pigs.

Saturday 28/1/1939.

Today we get all the cargo gear ready for workingout the ballast and taking on the cargo.

Geoff is invited into the saloon with his ukelele to entertain the after guard, and arrives back at the fo'c'sle in the late evening rather the worse for drink. He gives us a tune and a song or two and then becomes a bit argumentative, bordering on the bellicose, so I assist him to his bunk. He is off to sleep as soon as his head hits the sack and keeps the other lads of the port watch, Kulberg, Bjorkman and Lindross awake with his snoring. I am on watch and am bloody glad when I have to relieve the man at the wheel.

Sunday 29/1/1939.

It is blowing fairly hard today so we take in the royals and have two men at the wheel all day and night.

Monday 30/1/1939.

It is still blowing hard today and we are making good progress towards our destination, not very far to go now.

There are still two men at the wheel until night fall when the wind eases away a bit and we set the royals.

Tuesday 31/1/1939.

Steadily now we are approaching the land and there are many sea birds following in our wake and perching up in the rigging, a few of us get splashed with bird lime.

Around Bridlington Bay when I was a lad, this was supposed to be a sign of good luck but amongst some of my Finnish shipmates it did not appear to be such a good omen. At least, not by the amount of cursing that was hurled at the birds by those who managed to get whitewashed, it was "Satan, Satan, Satan, Pjevla Satan, Perkele kun minuu Vitutoa" and much more. But it didn't stop the birds fouling things up by the bucketful.

Wednesday 1/2/1939.

We make our landfall at about 1745 when we sight what we think to be Kangaroo Island and two smaller islands as we approach the entrance to the Spencer Gulf. Everybody now seems to be getting excited and most of the lads are having haircuts and shaving off their beards. Some of us surely look a bit odd as we are all suntanned or weather beaten, some of us to the point of being black-brown in colour, when the whiskers come off, the skin underneath is a much lighter shade. Happily a few days of Australian sunshine removes this pallid, sickly looking hue. The Mates have all put on clean white cap covers but so far Ragnar has not brought out his new uniform.

As dusk sets in the flashing light of a light house is a welcome sight after a voyage of around 14,000 miles, with never a sight of land once we cleared Rathlin Island on the 9/11/38. The crew members who live up for'ard are all crouching into our small quarters eagerly looking at the chart we proudly possess and checking on the islands we have sighted. There is much speculation and discussion and we now think that as our noon position was 35°6'S 136°5'E we are a little too close in to sight Kangeroo Island and the Navigators amongst us think the islands to be Thistle and Gambler which are situated right in the entrance to the Spencer Gulf.

The potatoes lasted a fair long time but for a couple of weeks now we have been having rice and what we call potato conserve, which is a type of potato flour and which is quite palatable. When dished up it takes the form and substance of mashed potatoes, very similar to that widely publicised product of the modern age called 'Smash' that is often advertised on T.V. This proves the point that there is nothing much new, it has mostly all been done before.

As the last of my old companions, the pigs, had sadly departed this life several weeks ago and been devoured forthwith, we are now eagerly looking forward to some fresh meat, vegetables and fruit.

We have in no way suffered any malnutrition on the voyage out as thanks to our steward Arno Stromberg and cook Rolf Forsman we have been quite adequately provided for, at least by long voyage windjammer standards.

So, by and large thanks to their very capable efforts, the strenuous exercise of pulley hauley by the "Armstrong patent method", the scrambling up aloft, the sun and the good clean salt air, we were all as fit as butchers dogs and all of us looking forward to setting foot on dry land once more. Not to mention of course eagerly looking forward to the delights, dubious, or otherwise we may be fortunate or unfortunate to encounter.

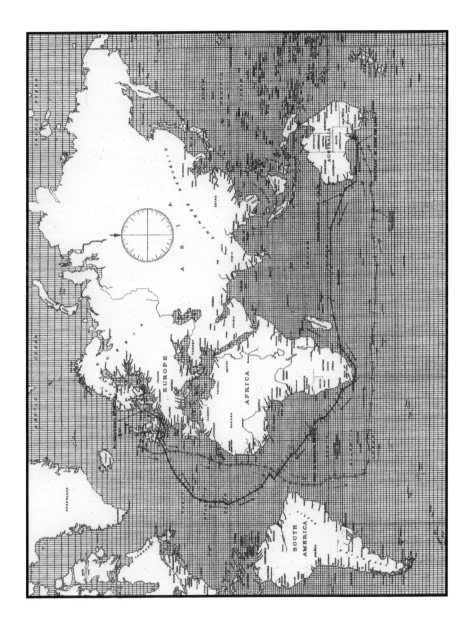

79

Wednesday 2/2/1939.

We sight Port Victoria about 0600 and commence to shorten sail and by 0830 we are all snugged down up aloft and are riding at anchor out at the ballast dumping grounds a few miles off the land.

So ends a passage of 86 days from Donaghadee to South Australia and happily by the grace of God we are all fit and healthy, having suffered nothing more than sea cracks (known by a rather more vulgar name by seamen) and salt water boils.

We are treated to a fine sight on our arrival as 'POMMERN', 'PAMIR', 'MOSHULU', and 'VIKING' are all riding at anchor, and 'LAWHILL' comes up from Port Lincoln about four hours later in the day.

All these vessels are owned by Captain Gustaf Erikson. All are big 4 masted barques and they represent nearly one half of the worlds latter day sailing vessels, which participate in the annual grain race.

We were not to know this at the time, but it was to be (sadly indeed) the last great concentration of commercial windjammers South Australia was ever to see.

When the coal and the oil run out, this type of vessel may emerge once more and again sail the 7 seas.

A happy thought indeed, but probably only a pipe dream

Self on the topgallant spars far right furling sail

PORT VICTORIA

On arrival at Port Victoria we anchor out at the ballast dumping grounds and the crew rig the gear for dumping the ballast.

The main yard was partially cock-billed and preventer wires shackled on to help take the strain. A gin block was shackled near the end of the yard arm from two wire pennants. Shackled between the fore and mainmasts hung another gin block, the gins each having a wire runner rove through and one runner is made fast to each winch barrel. A union purchase rig was obtained and the 'heavy gang' were sent down into the hold to start filling the baskets, which were then hauled up with great speed and upended over the ships side. "Plenty bloody hurry up now" as the donkeyman on one winch and a seaman on the other were trying to get the basket up, tipped and down into the hold again before the shovellers had got the next basket filled. Plenty muck, plenty sweat, plenty cursing, "Perkele", "Perkele", "Satan", "Satan" and a few choice epithets in English. These were thrown in by Geoff who was unlucky to be one of the unfortunates to be given a shovel, all this plus a lot of spurring on by the Mates who were working as hard as the rest of us.

I was the lucky one as I was made night watchman for the first week. This duty being a steady enough number but my problem was trying to sleep through the day with all the noise, the heat and the swarms of bloody flies. We worked out several hundreds of tons of ballast over the next few days.

The Mate showed me how to take bearings and if the wind comes away fresh, as it often seemed to do during the night, how to make regular checks on these bearings. Also, how to feel at the anchor cable to see if it was jumping and if so to call him immediately as she was probably dragging her anchor.

I had to get him out one night and he gave her another shackle or so of chain cable and from then on she held. My other duties being to ensure that the anchor lights were lit and clear and keeping the galley fire going and calling the cook at the appointed hour so he could get the coffee on.

I also had to call all hands at 0530 and take the coffee to both fo'c'sles and keep an eye on things in general.

On arrival off Port Victoria one of the hands had been sent aloft with the 'Q' flag of the International code, signifying we request Pratique. Which is to say that we required a licence to have dealings with the port on showing a clean bill of health. He made the flag fast to the mizzen Royal back stay a little way down so the flag could be clearly seen and would not wrap itself around the mast. Before sundown on this first day I was sent up to bring the flag down but when I got aloft I found the flag must have been made fast to the stay with a couple of slippery hitches, as it had worked its way down and had taken a couple of turns round the stay. I went down after it, cleared it from the stay and untied the hitches but could not get back up again to the royal yard in order to come down to the deck in the orthodox manner. Instead, as the flag was blowing in the breeze, I had to take it in my teeth and descend with it in this fashion 170 odd feet, hand over hand down the backstay to the deck.

I think I must have gone up half a notch in the opinion of Mr Anderson the 2nd, Mate, for unbeknown to me he had watched the whole procedure. When I arrived back on the deck he had a wide grin on his face and I think I detected a slight glint of (not admiration) but approval in his eye. However, I bet he would have given me "hell" if I had lost the bloody flag over the side.

Whilst on the subject of flags, the old man was very meticulous with regard to the Finnish ensign. At sunrise it was hoisted and at sunset it was lowered (to the minute) and though the poop deck of 'OLIVEBANK' was spotless, the ensign had not to come into contact with it. More than one night watchman that voyage got bawled out regarding this matter.

Shortly after our arrival at the ballast grounds the crew rigged the accommodation ladder over the starboard side, abreast of the break of the poop and a little way for'ard of it they rigged a mooring boom, to which were moored the ships motor boat and pram when they were not in use.

The motor boat was used more or less daily when weather conditions allowed taking the old man and crew members ashore and on occasion paying visits to the other sailing vessels anchored there.

Part of my job as night watchman was to make sure that the two boats remained secure and I used to check them every hour or so as the wind sometimes came away quite strong during the night.

On making a routine check at about 4 a.m. one morning I was very startled to see that the motor boat was adrift and steadily moving down wind away from 'OLIVEBANK' and was by now some 150 ft. astern of her. I straight away ran into the forward fo'c'sle and roused Julius Henriksson who was motor boatman and whilst he threw on a few articles of clothing I dashed aft and woke the 2nd Mate and told him what was amiss. I also called the cook who quite naturally pulled a long face and uttered a few choice oaths at being awakened a good hour sooner than usual. However, I felt I had to make sure he was up in good time to get the coffee on the stove and by the same token to make sure the 2nd Mate was up and about and ready to drink it, as I was still smarting a little over the other coffee episode.

Henriksson and I then dashed on to the mooring boom and down into the pram and set off with a pair of oars apiece to chase and hopefully catch the motor boat, which was now drifting steadily away down wind and was several hundred yards distant as wind and tide had got hold of her. Although she was not a big boat she presented a fair amount of freeboard and was thus catching a lot of wind.

We had not been pulling for long before we had a visitor swimming fairly close alongside, a shark of probably seven or eight feet in length, joined a few minutes later by another of the same size. Not a very pleasant state of affairs as the pram was of no great dimensions and had little enough freeboard. The presence of those two creatures spurred us on to greater efforts which might have earned us a gold had we been sculling in the Olympics.

Presently we came alongside the motor boat, made fast to her and scrambled aboard, into what was a much safer place.

After several attempts to get the motor going and much foul language in several tongues we gave up, shipped an oar apiece and started to pull back towards 'OLIVEBANK' which by now was a long way off. After much heaving, grunting and sweating we decided we could not make it, so we altered course a little and started to pull across wind and make for 'LAWHILL' but we were carried past her and finally fetched up alongside 'VIKING' and made fast to her.

We went aboard and were given coffee which was very welcome and much enjoyed by us. A little later we reported to her 1st Mate who arranged for their motor boat to tow us back to 'OLIVEBANK' after breakfast.

Nothing was said to me but I fear poor Julius got a rousting, for he had a hang dog expression for days.

When the required amount of ballast had been dumped we moved nearer inshore to take on the first of the wheat cargo to act as stiffening. Meanwhile the hold and bilges etc which had been under ballast were cleaned and prepared for loading.

At Port Victoria there was a wooden jetty of some length but large vessels could not go alongside, therefore the cargo was brought out to the deep water vessels in small auxiliary ketches.

Wheat ketch Capella coming alongside Olivebank 1939

This method of course entailed much handling of the wheat, as it was first brought into the port by lorry and probably horse drawn carts from the surrounding countryside and piled up in great stacks all over the place. Presently it was loaded into light trucks on a narrow gauge track which ran the length of the jetty. There was no engine to move the trucks, they were either man handled or horse drawn.

The sacks of grain were next tipped down shutes into the holds of the ketches and brought out to the waiting vessels, whose own gear then lifted the slings of bagged wheat aboard.

The wheat ketch Falie coming up to Olivebank 1939
photo Jeff Yates

The names of almost all of the ketches which served us were: 'FALIE', 'CAPELLA', 'LEPRENA', 'HAROLD', 'COURABIE', 'ALERT', 'ENA', and' GERARD'

Fred Boy at the helm of the Falie 1939 photo Jeff Yates

The cargo was distributed around the hold, tier by tier, by the gang of about 8 or 10 'lumpers' who came out to 'OLIVEBANK' and lived aboard all through the period of loading.

The method used by these rough tough lads was to build up a platform of bagged wheat about shoulder high in the bottom of the hold onto which the slings of bags were loaded. Two men would be on this platform and their job was to loose off the slings and stand the bags on end so that the lads who were carrying could drop the bags across their shoulders and trot off with them to the appointed place. This was really hard graft, as all our cargo came aboard through No's 2 and 3 hatches and then had to be humped the rest of the way.

I don't know what the 'lumpers' wages were, but it was not enough for the effort they expended, of that I feel sure. I think the bags would be 12 stone in weight or 168lbs and humping those all day was no mean feat.

Every so often some of the bags would be cut open and the grain would be allowed to bleed out down into the spaces between the stowed bags to give a firm solid stow.

Planks of timber were lashed between the upright stanchions in the hold to form a wooden centre line bulkhead, to act as shifting boards.

The language of the Glasgow dockers last October when I joined 'OLIVEBANK' was indeed fluent with every second or third word beginning with the letter 'F' but they had nothing on these wild Australian boys who were fluent and poetic. Past masters in the use of invective, they made the language of the Glasgow lads sound like play school stuff.

So much then for loading grain Port Victoria style, a far cry indeed from the great grain ports of Canada and the U.S.A. where pre-war, a vessel could load a 10,000 ton wheat cargo, loading simultaneously down 5 hatches in about 8 hours.

They unloaded at the same speed in the U.K. and on the continent. (No doubt much faster than that in this day and age.

The Spencer Gulf had many Ports which handled grain. Some were just anchorages such as Port Victoria. In some a vessel could get alongside a quay or jetty to load, as at Port Lincoln.

Through the years the old windjammers loaded at Port Lincoln, Port Victoria, Port Germein, Port Broughton, Port Augusta, Wallaroo, and I believe also at Port Pirie and Whyalla but in the loading for the last grain race 1938/1939 only three Ports were used, namely Port Germein, Port Lincoln, and Port Victoria.

After several days of loading we move out once more to the ballast grounds and work out the remainder of the ballast, which again takes a few days.

No such luck as last time for me this time, as I am now in the heavy gang and I am presented with a bloody shovel and this time I get my fair share of sweat and muck.

When the last of the ballast has been taken out we raise the anchor and return to the loading area.

On the way in we nearly have a disaster, as the wind suddenly comes away very strong and 'OLIVEBANK' for some reason or other at this time is very slow to answer the helm and we nearly go ashore on a small island. The anchor really goes down with a roar, but you could hear the Old Man's roar which was louder by far. That little episode caused some commotion and really broke up the monotony.

The gang of 'lumpers' and their Tally Clerk were pleasant enough lads and lived aboard until we had completed the loading and we struck up quite a friendship with them all. The crew rigged some sails to act as a shelter between the break of the poop and the after end of our deck house and underneath the lifeboats.

The 'lumpers' brought their own bedrolls etc. with them and the ship provided the food and they seemed happy enough.

One of them caught a small shark one day and he told me it was a grey nurse. It was about 2 ft 6ins in length and apparently this species are real killers when grown. To demonstrate he gave it a piece of wood about two inches wide and half an inch thick. The shark clamped down on the wood with a vice-like action and by the sheer strength of its jaws it snapped the wood in two.

The 'lumper' cut off its tail and threw it overboard and it was only a matter of minutes before its brothers and sisters had devoured it.

Now that all the ballast was out and the loading going on at a steady pace when wind and weather allowed it, most of the crew was now over the side on stages chipping and scraping away at the rust scars and giving the scaled sections of plating a few coats of red lead. This was followed by a coat or two of black paint. The pram was in great demand at this time for getting around the rust patches close to the water line.

The cargo was now all being loaded in at No.3 hatch and with a slightly different rig for to save on coal one winch only was now being used.

The Cro'jack yard was partially cockbilled and rigged with preventer wires and a skeleton gin block shackled up at the yard arm. Through this block was rove a long length of three and a half inch or four inch manilla rope with a light skeleton gin block attached to one end of it, through this gin the wire runner was rove. This manilla rope acted as an outhaul for the runner and empty sling when there was no great weight on it and it was manually hauled out until the runner plumbed the hatch of the ketch.

On hooking on a loaded sling the load was lifted clear of the ketch and slightly higher than 'OLIVEBANK'S' bulwarks and then with several turns of outhaul round a bollard it was allowed to surge so that the sling load came in board and was then lowered down into the hold. The winch on top of the galley was being used for this operation, with the runner leading first from the winch up to a block between the two masts and thence through the skeleton gin attached to the outhaul.

The donkeyman was kept busy keeping a good head of steam and oiling the winch, whilst little Halpo Alanen was winch man almost all of the time. He was a great character, with laughing mischievous eyes and a little dark moustache which he had retained when he shaved off his beard. He had a fairly deep voice and was a merry little man full of fun who used to try really hard to converse with us in English.

Lennart Henrikson was in charge of the outhaul rope and did most of the heaving himself, though I seem to recall from time to time some of us were detailed off to give him a hand. This surely was hard graft, standing there for hours in the blazing sunshine with little or no shade hauling on that outhaul every couple of minutes or so but I never heard him complain.

Lennart was a quiet lad in his mid twenties, medium height with a big barrel of a chest and very powerful arms. Very studious and conscientious and a little bit on the shy side with us British, as he spoke very little English but a pleasant lad indeed, and though a quiet man, he would have been a hard one to tackle in a fight. By the time we finished the loading, his chest and arms seemed inches bigger.

The loading went on steadily as far as wind and weather and availability of ketches allowed, sometimes we would be held up a day or two, as from time to time we had some very high winds and rough seas which made it impossible for the ketches to come alongside.

When we were ashore we used to pray for the wind, to increase so that we may be weather bound and not be able to get back to the ship. This did happen on the odd occasion, though why in hell we should want to have done this is now beyond me for we were usually broke and there was little to do in Port Victoria anyway.

Port Victoria was only a small place. It boasted a jetty, the Wauraltee or Waraltee Hotel, (in which bar we spent much of our hard earned money) was about the first building one encountered after stepping off the jetty. A very wide main street, unsurfaced in those days, with wooden buildings with corrugated iron roofs up both sides of the street. Many of these buildings had a wooden board walk and hitching rails in front of them, like one tends to see in films of the Wild West, though I do not recollect seeing very many horses moored up to these rails.

There was a Church and either a Church or Village Hall where the crews of the sailing vessels were very kindly entertained by the warm hearted residents. These good people organised dances and film shows for us once in a while.

On the opposite side of the street was a large general store which sold everything and anything, and was owned by a family called Trehearne, whose older members hailed from down around Cornwall. I can recall the very first time I went in to make a purchase, one of the older members of the family, on hearing my voice looked at me and said, "Which part of Yorkshire do you come from?" I must have retained much of my local way of speech even after several months of speaking international seaman's language. I used to often go to the store just to chat to Mr Trehearne who was a kindly and pleasant gentleman and who, despite having been in Australia for many years, always seemed very interested to hear news of what was going on in the U.K.

There was a small Post Office and up at the top of the street a small cafe. I do not recall any more shops though I feel that there may have been one or two small ones but as I recall everything was centered round the one main street.

Port Victoria was just a small port and probably did not see any other large vessels apart from the old windjammers from one grain season to the next. It was truly rural and of course at this time of year after the harvest, was all brown and sun baked with very little greenery. As far as I know it had no ladies of easy virtue, or other dubious delights, to offer to tired and lonely toilers of the deep. It had a nice beach and we sometimes went there to swim and though it was probably not too safe from sharks, it was I feel, reasonably so, if one did not venture too far out into deep water. It was most certainly not safe to swim from the ships out at the anchorage, for there were sharks in plenty out there to be sure.

Port Victoria had one policeman, but the force was doubled to two for the period of time it took to get the local wheat shipped out.

The peace of this little township would often be disturbed at night by some of we drunken idiots who had come ashore and swilled down a few pints before the pub closed its doors at 1800 hours. Then, if we had money enough, we would buy a bottle of plonk (or 'red biddy', as it was sometimes called,) which was just cheap Australian wine, costing in those days 2/6 or half a crown (twelve and a half pence in today's coinage). This potion was indeed a savage type of drink especially to us lads who had not tasted strong drink since we left the U.K. apart from the odd celebratory tot that we had been given aboard 'OLIVEBANK' on high days and holidays.

It worked in many different ways, to say the least, on us toilers of the deep. It made some happy, some morose, some violently ill, some just wanted to go to sleep and a few wanted to tear the place apart. In many cases it appeared to inflame many of the lads into thinking that they were world champion pugilists.

Several fights were fought down that main street of Port Victoria and many old scores were settled, usually between crew members from, the different vessels but not always - sometimes it was a needle match between two lads off the one vessel.

Happily I never once heard of any involvement with or by any of the local populace, who had the great good sense to leave us alone and let us lick our own wounds.

A gentleman called John Scott-Todd was Agent for 'OLIVEBANK' and also for 'MOSHULU'. He was in charge of the shipping of the wheat cargo. He probably acted as agent for all the vessels there but on this point I am not sure. Mrs Scott-Todd and John were very hospitable people and they very kindly entertained me up at their home on several occasions. The table would be filled with fine things to eat and here I sampled and enjoyed real Australian hospitality.

I rather fancy that these good people entertained many of the British lads off the several ships, and on at least one occasion I met up with Eric Newby who was an apprentice in 'MOSHULU' and who, several years later, wrote "The Last Grain Race" which is quite an hilarious account of his round voyage in sail.

John Scott-Todd took me to visit a large farm several miles from Port Victoria. It was a cattle station and a very sizeable place that employed a lot of aborigines and was in fact a settlement complete with its own school.

It would appear that some of the native children were very good at art and one of the lads who would be no more than about 10 years old drew a very good picture for me of two boxers in the ring, which sadly I do not now possess.

The young lady who taught these youngsters expressed a wish to come aboard 'OLIVEBANK' to look around, so on my return to the ship I approached Captain Granith, who readily gave his permission. The kindly man that he was, he told me he would arrange to have this young lady transported in our motor boat and that she and myself, were invited to take a meal with him in the saloon.

This proposed visit unfortunately did not take place owing to some unforeseen circumstances developing, which prevented the young lady getting to Port Victoria.

Needless to say I was very disappointed and I feel Captain Granith was also as he took great pride and pleasure in having people aboard to look round his ship.

******

I managed to get a few days leave in lieu of payment for some overtime I had worked and managed a short visit of about three days to Adelaide.

A lorry used to run between Adelaide and Port Victoria once or twice a week bringing various supplies. The driver used to drive through the night and on payment of £1 Australian money would convey you to Adelaide and return.

I took the trip with him and spent most of the night watching out for Puff-adders and other snakes which he said could often be seen crossing the road but I was out of luck in that respect, as we never spotted a single one.

Port Adelaide 1930's Photo Jeff Yates

Adelaide proved to be a very pleasant place, a very clean city with many trees, gardens and nice shops. When built, it was a mile square with all the roads and streets being at right angles to each other. However, by 1939 it had extended beyond its original boundaries quite a bit. I passed my time having a good look around, paid a visit to the Dentist for a filling and a visit to one of the local Hospitals to visit one of the Finnish boys off one of the other ships who happened to have had an accident, happily he was making a good recovery.

I also sampled fresh nectarines and passion fruit which, in those days, you could not get fresh in the U.K. My mother, who was born in Melbourne, often used to talk of these two varieties of fruit and how pleasant they were to eat.

It was also my good fortune to befriend a local lad named Jim Daly, who was a lorry driver doing local deliveries in and around Adelaide. I spent much of my time with him riding around and seeing the sights.

Amongst other places he took me was to a snake farm where you were allowed to handle some of the non-venomous varieties but I settled for just a brief touch of a small Boa.

I was in touch with Jim Daly until, after the end of the war but sadly we have now lost touch. He was fighting in the Western desert with the Australian forces and used to write frequently to my Mother at this time.

******

During our stay in Port Victoria much ship's maintenance was carried out, rust scaling, red leading, and painting the hull, general cleaning up of paintwork, brass work etc. on deck. As the bags of wheat steadily rise in the hold we are still kept busy rigging sweat boards and wrapping the stanchions with strips of burlap.

Donkeyman imparted a very odd bit of information today. It appears that in some previous ship, he had been unlucky enough to have a problem with pubic lice, as had several of the other crew members and there had been a great demand for the limited supply of mercurial ointment. So much so, that by the time Donkey required some, stocks had run out, so he soaked a lot of old fag ends in paraffin over-night and applied some of the mixture next day. He said it worked wonders and after a few applications he was rid of the lice. He did also say that the paraffin was a bit savage and tended to burn the tender skin.

Coming back aboard one evening after a few hours ashore, there were only four of us in the motor boat - the Mate, the passenger, Julius Henriksson and myself. The two former had both had a good drink but the latter two were cold sober (probably because we were broke). Half way back to 'OLIVEBANK' the passenger must have mumbled something which offended the Mate, for a fight ensued which didn't last very long as the Mate soon got the upper hand but they almost capsized the boat. It was a good job it was a beamy little craft.

Ashore one evening, and no doubt after several drinks, a tree uprooting contest took place down the main street, where there were some young saplings growing. Chippy who was usually a quiet chap and big Tor Sontag seemed to be representing 'OLIVEBANK' and there were several boys off some of the other ships. They made great efforts between them to uproot some of these trees single handed as it were, with one man to one tree and of course spurred on to greater efforts by we cheering spectators.

A few of these young trees were damaged and to our child-like minds it was, I suppose all great fun at the time - a view I would not share today.

A few days later several of the contestants were served with summonses and hauled before the court at a place called Maitland and were duly fined. Unfortunately someone got the idea that I had told the Police who the culprits were - which was quite incorrect, as I had no reason at all to do this. When I went ashore a few nights later, I was confronted by a crew member off another ship, who I did not even know and he accused me of telling the Police and wanted to engage me in mortal combat. I was just about to oblige him when several crew members off various other ships, who had gathered around, broke it up and stopped the fight before it got underway, which I feel was very surprising, as mostly we enjoyed watching a scrap and seeing some blood flow.

A fairly well known writer of sailing vessel stories A.A. Hurst who was a crew member in one of the other vessels S.V. 'POMMERN' and whom I had met but briefly, wrote something of this happening in one of his books 'The Call of High Canvas'. He made a few derogatory remarks about both Geoff Robertshaw and myself which were to say the least of it ill-founded and not worthy of him at all. He must not have felt too sure of his facts as he does not name us but simply refers to us as the two men who came from near Halifax.

During the month of February, 'POMMERN' went up to Port Germein to pick up some cargo and then returned to Port Victoria to complete loading.

'VIKING' was the first to finish loading and she sailed for the U.K. around the middle of the month.

A little later 'LAWHILL' went down to Port Lincoln to top off her cargo.

By about the first week in March the remaining four vessels were nearly completely loaded and when one went ashore it was very noticeable how the huge stacks of bagged wheat, which had seemingly been stacked all over Port Victoria had dwindled so that very few remained.

'PAMIR' sailed on the 8.3.39 followed by 'MOSHULU' on the 11.3.39 and it is much quieter ashore now with only two vessels left out at the anchorage.

Geoff Robertshaw left us and I had a letter to say he had joined a steamer named 'CAPE HOWE'. The Rev. Jon Robertshaw, nephew of Geoff Robertshaw and a very good friend of mine states in the obituary that he prepared for the 'Cape Horner' in January 1984 that Geoff did in fact return to the U.K. in a city line vessel, which will no doubt be correct and that Geoff was in fact on his way back to the U.K. by the time I received his letter.

One of our other crew members tried to jump ship, aided a little by me, as he wanted to try his luck in Australia.

Fortunately or unfortunately, as the case may be, he was picked up by the police in Adelaide and escorted back aboard in due course. I am afraid it proved a costly venture for the lad, for much of the expense incurred was deducted from his earnings.

Donkeyman, Vaino Makinen has been ill for some little while and appears very drawn and haggard and has lost much weight and a few days before we sail he is put ashore and goes into hospital, so we have to leave him behind.

'OLIVEBANK' completed her loading on 16th March and we said farewell to our cheerful old mates, the lumpers, as they go ashore for the last time.

I am invited to the Scott-Todd household for a farewell meal, but the Mate says "no more shore leave", as it is too near sailing time. He probably thought that if I got ashore I might make my exit, which was in fact the thought farthest from my mind.

The old Man had taken me to task after the other lad had been brought back by the police and asked me if I intended to desert (which I did not). The Captain told me that if it was my intention to stay in Australia he would arrange for me (as a British citizen) to gain legal entry and would pay me off thus saving a lot of hassle and expense all round.

About the time we completed loading, an aged steamer named 'QUORNA' brought us out our stores for the homeword voyage, foodstuffs, and a few ships stores, which included some bolts of canvas, coal, water and three live pigs.

One or two crew members either off 'QUORNA' or off one of the last ketches to come alongside were on our deck. One of these lads, a thick set, dark skinned heavily tattooed character, sporting a wide brimmed Australian bush hat was spotted by our Mate walking up the deck with a bolt of canvas under his arm. The Mate shouted for him to stop, which order was completely ignored by the would be thief, on which Ragnar charged up the deck, confronted him and relieved him of the bolt of canvas and in no uncertain terms ordered the would be miscreant off the ship, who complied without further ado.

Needless to say some of 'OLIVEBANKS' crew, myself included, were very disappointed at this for we had anticipated a battle royal.

Fred Boy holding life buoy of Gerard

HOMEWARD BOUND

Monday 20/3/1939.

Today we have a favourable wind to get us out of the Spencer Gulf and both 'OLIVEBANK' and 'POMMERN' weigh anchor at the same time, get some sail on and start to move away down the Gulf. The wind presently freshens and as we approach the open sea we run into a fairly heavy swell.

We are now deep loaded with about 4,400 tons of wheat so it probably won't be long now before we get some water on deck.

During our last 2 days at Port Victoria whilst waiting for a favourable wind, everything has been made doubly secure. The four hatches have all been well battened down, and on top of the tarpaulins has been laid a cover of 3" planking, over which are laid locking bars, which in turn are secured by turn-buckles to ring bolts in the deck.

Life lines of wire have been stretched taut by capstan and run from the fo'c'sle head to the poop. From these life lines are rigged, thwart ships, lengths of 3" rope, which gave us all something extra to grab at when the need arises.

'OLIVEBANK' and 'POMMERN' are running steadily and up to now are keeping fairly close to each other. At about 1800 hours we pass a Standard oil tanker - 'HENRY DUNDAS'- heading in up the Spencer Gulf.

Tuesday 21/3/1939.

This day we see the last of the land and we are on the open sea once more. 'POMMERN' is hull down and away to southward and presumably trying to find the westerlies which should speed her and us on the way to Cape Horn. We have our old friends the albatross with us once more.

Wednesday 22/3/1939.

We have a fresh, following wind and are making good headway and have tacked and taken in stay sails.

A big following sea is running and we are rolling and taking water on deck.

Course NW by W three quarters W

Thursday 2 3/3/1939.

A good stiff following wind and fairly-big sea coming up from astern, still rolling and taking water on deck but not in any great amount. We sight 'POMMERN' once more she is on our heels and gaining steadily. It now appears that neither of us have found the Westerlies and that both Masters have decided to run home west about, via Cape of Good Hope. This to some of us is something of a disappointment as we wanted to travel the Cape Horn road.

Olivebank from Pommern.   Photo Len Townend.

Friday 24/3/1939.

At daybreak 'POMMERN' is still with us and is catching up with us fairly rapidly. The helmsmen are all getting bawled at and told in no uncertain manner to hold the course and there is a fair amount of "Satan, Satan, Helvete and Djevla" from the 2nd Mate. When I relieve the wheel, for my benefit, I get it in English "Jesus Christ can't you hold the bloody course Townend?" However, the sea and wind conditions make it almost impossible to keep her steady.

A snag develops which causes some more foul language mid-morning when the mizzen royal starboard brace carries away. Fortunately no other damage, and it is soon relieved, shortly afterwards a fore upper topsail buntline parts but no real problem with this. The weather is now very dull and we get some rain.

'POMMERN' draws alongside about 1030 a.m. and we take some photos. The Old Man speaks to her officers through the megaphone and by noon she is drawing ahead of us. Both vessels making a fine sight, with just about every stitch of canvas set.

'POMMERN' was baldheaded, so did not cross any royal yards but her masts appeared to be near enough as lofty as those of 'OLIVEBANK' although her rig was not as pleasing to the eye. (Old hands of 'POMMERN' may not agree).

A deep laden British tanker steams right between the two old windjammers and exchanges signals with us both. She is bound for one of the Australian ports and is steaming right into the teeth of the wind and sea and is making very heavy weather of it with her decks continually awash.

Saturday 25/3/1939.

Lady Day, a holiday. No maintenance work today just normal watch keeping and routine duties. The wind is strong and there is a big sea running so there are two men at the wheel. The old ship is charging along in fine style and still taking a lot of water on deck, the life lines now coming into use quite often.

Course NW quarter W

'POMMERN' is out of sight and no doubt is somewhere up ahead. Most of the hands have again had the hair shaved off their heads and have once more started to grow beards. All hands got a good tot of rum this afternoon and somehow or other Timberman managed to get a little drunk. He is a great character but can still speak only a few words of English.

Shaven heads Albin Bjorkman, Borje Kullberg,Gunnar Lindroos.

By night fall the wind has died right away and there is a big swell which is causing us to roll heavily. Steering is by the wind and we are hardly making any headway, it's uncanny how the wind has dropped away so rapidly.

Sunday 26/3/1939.

A very red dawn this morning and it soon comes very dull and starts to rain steadily. There is little or no wind and we clew up all courses and leave them hanging by the clews and buntlines, this way they are not slatting and banging and chafing against the rigging so much. We try to take her on to the other tack but have so little way that it is impossible to bring her round.

102

The second mate is a bit edgy and is giving us two blasts of his whistle at the slightest pretext, take a pull on this brace, ease off that buntline a bit, set the spanker sheet tight. Everyone is as mad as hell and there is a lot of mumbling and cursing going on in a quiet manner.

I have the wheel from 1700 to 1800 hrs and I have a very exciting time.

There has been little wind all day but a big oily swell running, we are on the starboard tack and suddenly without any warning at all we get a strong blow coming from the port side and we are taken fairly and squarely aback.

The wind is so strong it starts driving us astern. I have several anxious moments at the wheel but not half as anxious as those which the second Mate is experiencing for the poor chap gets so worked up that for a few minutes he doesn't seem to know port from starboard. Eventually we get her round on the other tack, nearly carrying away the mainmast or at least some of the main top-hamper in the process through letting the braces run free.

Happily all ends well and no damage done.

The wind holds steady and strong for about half, an hour and then dies away as quickly as it came.

The Mate bought a rifle in Port Victoria and he and the other officers have had a happy time potting at bottles and cans which they have been throwing overboard.

Monday 27/3/1939.

More wind today, steering by the wind and a heavy sea running, into which we are heading and at times we are shipping water over the fo'c'sle head.

At 2345 hrs we get two whistles and clew up the main royal, as the wind has caused one of the royal sheets to part and the sail is whipping and lashing like something possessed. Laakso and Englund go aloft to make it fast.

Tuesday 28/3/1939.

More rain today and over the last few days we have collected enough rain water by spreading spare sails around, that we have managed to fill the starboard tank up for'ard, so we should have enough water to wash in for some time.

Chippy has now got much of the re-planking of the deck completed and we are now employed with the task of planeing it level with double handed planes, two men to a plane. (No sanding machines in that day and age.)

Wednesday 29/3/1939.

Today there is a steady following breeze with nice, warm sunshine and really pleasant weather.

Mostly we are occupied now with that soul destroying seamans hell, holystoning, the process being;

1. Where there is new planking it is first leveled down with hand planes.

2. The deck is well wetted and sand is scattered over it.

3. A large deck bear, made up of a sand filled canvas bag covered with rope worked into a half hitching so that the bag was completely encased, is dragged up and down the deck by at least four of us as it was a weighty contraption.

4. The next process was to use a large slab of smooth sand stone weighing about three quarters of a hundredweight (38kgrm) to which were attached two long handles of wood, similar in shape to old type lawn mower handles. This was operated by two men on a pull- push basis doing a small section of deck at a time.

5. Lastly out came the "prayer books", small hand holystones and down you went on your knees amongst the wet sand to give the decking its final smooth off.

A long, laborious, tedious and uncomfortable occupation to say the least and it went on for a long time when weather permitted.

A long, laborious, tedious and uncomfortable occupation

We are now well past Cape Leeuwin.

Course N.N.W. half W.

Thursday 30/3/1939.

We make a good steady pace with a fairly strong breeze and are heading up a little into the Indian Ocean.

We have taken down all life lines and stowed them away and have once more started to send down the heavy weather canvas and bend lighter sails. Kangas and Julias Henriksson are now both on day work and are busy repairing trade wind sails. Timberman is also on day work and is busy scaling and cleaning the donkey boiler inside and out and preparing it for painting.

Course N.N.W. half W.

Position 31° - 35'S. 108° - 47'E.

Friday 31/3/1939. to Monday 3/4/1939.

A steady breeze prevails through this period with much sunshine and we complete the changing of all sails.

Tuesday 4/4/1939.

Today there is scarcely a puff of wind and so we get plenty of drill at the braces trying to catch every catspaw.

The 3rd Mate known as Treon is now also on daywork and is busy with palm and needle along with Kangas and Henriksson. On the outward passage he was nicknamed "Gamla Perkele" he has now earned himself a new name "Gamla Tre Plus", (Old three plus) as he is now informing all those who do not carry out their duties to his satisfaction that he hopes that at some time or other they will catch syphilis which will progress until it becomes tertiary. He doesn't really mean this as he always says it with a merry twinkle in his eye. He spends much of his free time playing with the ship's cat and, on the odd occasion, I have seen him giving some boxing instruction to the 2nd Mate.

Course NNW half W.

Wednesday 5/4/1939,

We have a following wind and roll heavily for much of the day and consequently we take a fair amount of water over both gunwales and the deck is constantly awash. The freeing ports are playing a merry tune as they open to let the water out and then close with a bang as she rolls the other way.

No need at this stage of the voyage to wet down the decks before sun up and again at sundown to keep the planking moist, which under dry conditions is a twice daily routine job.

We sight another sailing ship around mid-morning well away to port. By 1530 we are abreast of her and it proves to be the 'LAWHILL'.

Signals are exchanged and we learn that she left Port Lincoln on 15th March. We steadily draw ahead of her and she is hull down as darkness descends.

106

'LAWHILL' was rigged in an unconventional manner she, like 'POMMERN' did not carry Royals. Her lower masts and top masts being one pole and the top gallant masts were fitted abaft the top masts, the jigger mast also being one pole.

Course N.W. quarter W.

Thursday 6/4/1939.

Wind and sea have eased away and we are once more hard at it with the bloody holystones and sand. A beautiful sunny day and 'OLIVEBANK' is making about 7 Knots.

Good Friday 7/4/1939.

Today is a holiday - no work today other than normal watch keeping and routine jobs - such as pig pen cleaning etc. It is a lovely warm day and steady breeze and we are still making 7 to 8 knots.

I spend all morning washing and airing clothes.

We all receive a good tot of brandy at noon.

Position 25°S 92° E

Saturday 8/4/1939.

A steady breeze and fine sunny weather, 'OLIVEBANK' is making steady progress at 7 to 9 knots with little bracing and pulley haul at this time.

Today we work with the holystones all day.

Chippy is making wooden buckets (cooper style) out of oak staves, brass bound, with rope handles finished off with either Mathew Walker or Stopper knots, a really artistic job when finished. Like many of the Scandinavians he is past master when working with wood.

Chippy and the steward killed a pig this afternoon, very humane, stunned it with a hammer and then bled it. This method conforms to British Standards of slaughter. Very little mess as the cook caught most of the blood for blood pancakes. The pig was then immersed in a tub of scalding water, and all the hair scraped off, finally it was hung up, gutted and then halved. It was just like they do it in my uncles slaughter house in Brighouse, apart from the method of stunning which he now does by electric current.

Sunday 9/4/1939 and Monday 10/4/1939. Easter.

We have a holiday on both days. Once again there are only the normal watch-keeping duties to perform.

Blood pancakes for breakfast and very nice too, also fresh pork for both mid-day and evening meals.

A steady breeze and fine weather with much washing and airing of clothing which got wet in the early stages of the voyage home.

Many of the lads have been working on their models whilst the ship has remained on a steady course with little or no rolling. Per Finnerman started his model during 1937/38. It is beautiful - about a metre in length and just about everything works, yards brace round and even the sheaves in the larger blocks work, a real masterpiece and one which he can be truly proud of. He has even made a large wooden case like a suitcase in which to store it. We are making a steady 8 knots.

Course NW. a quarter W.

Tuesday 11/4/1939.

Steady following wind. Back on our knees again today with the prayer books, we shall all be glad to see the end of this bloody job.

Course NW three quarters N

Position 25° S   81° E

Thursday 13/4/1939

Position. 25° S. 74° E.

Friday 14/4/1939

Position. 25° S. 71° 46' E.

Saturday 15/4/1939.

Today there is a strong wind once more and we have a fair amount of water on deck and I somehow manage to get washed across the deck and fetch up hard against a freeing port giving my shoulder a hefty whack.

We take in the cro'jack and gaff topsail and I go up to make the latter fast. It is just about the worst sail on the ship to take in as it is usually a single handed job and there is little support up on the jigger mast. You have to wrap your legs round a stay and grapple as best you can with that kicking fighting canvas. On this occasion it proved too much and the 2nd Mate sent up Valter Englund to bear a hand. Valter is a very quiet lad, very reticent but he grunts a lot and spends much time cursing the wind, the sail, the second Mate for sending him up aloft and me for not being able to manage by myself.

Course NW. three quarters N.

Wednesday 19/4/1939.

Great jubilation today - we have finished with the holy stones and put them away in the lockers and have oiled the deck with linseed oil to which has been added a slight touch of red lead and it really looks good.

Position. 25° S 58° 18' E.

Thursday 20/4/1939.

We have now started chipping rust and red leading wherever there is rust, deck houses, bulwarks, scuppers, etc. Wind holding steady.

Saturday 22/4/1939.

Position. 26° S. 50° E.

Sunday 23/4/1939.

A heavy rainstorm this afternoon, the wind shifts suddenly and we get taken aback but fortunately no damage done, though there was much shouting of orders and the Mate registers his disapproval with one of his cap stamping efforts but the Old Man tells him to calm down.

Monday 24/4/1939. - Friday 28/4/1939.

Wind and sea are confused most of this period and we get a lot of sail drill, as we have to tack at fairly regular intervals all week and steering by-the-wind most of the time.

Friday before noon we had a large water spout cross very close astern which caused much turbulence on the seas surface and in the atmosphere.

Saturday 29/4/1939.

A very bad squall this morning and all hands are called out to shorten sail. The main upper topsail and lower to' gallant are blown to shreds, followed in very rapid succession by 11 more sails, topsails, to'gallants a royal, and several staysails, all reduced to ribbons before we can do anything to save them. For a short while the air was full of flying shreds of canvas and all that remains of these sails now are rags and tatters and the bolt ropes. The sails were the older fair weather sails though they had withstood much weather but this sudden and savage onslaught of wind proved too much.

We have the lee rail under water until we can get more canvas off her.

It remains squally all day and by afternoon we have bent two fresh topsails and three staysails and have sent down all the rags and tatters. We are now running under storm canvas.

Nasty weather at the moment and everybody and everything very wet.

Position. 29° S. 36° E.

Sunday 30/4/1939.

A steamer passes us about 0100 hours and messages are exchanged by morse lamps it is heading the same way as ourselves.

At 0730 the German steamer 'LAHN' overtakes us and she gives us three blasts on her whistle and a dip of the Swastika (little did I know how soon I was to learn to hate that bloody ensign and all that it stood for).

Monday 1/5/1939.

Very little wind and nearly becalmed for some of the day. All hands are now hard at work bending new sails and trying to make good the near mishap of last Saturday. I go up with some of the others to bend a new fore royal. Much grumbling by us all and we curse last Saturdays weather very vehemently as today is May Day and a recognized holiday. We should not grumble about the work, as we are lucky that no one was killed or injured, or that 'OLIVEBANK' did not go over on her beam ends. Had it been the heavy duty canvas that had been aloft and had it withstood this savage squall, things may have been a lot worse.

Sailing by-the-wind in light airs.

Position. 29°S. 35° 66'E.

Friday 5/5/1939.

We have had light airs and rain this past few days and have had plenty of heave-ho, as we have been changing tack fairly regularly, two, three and sometimes four times daily.

A few of the lads are in the sail locker busy with palm and needle and the rest of us are down in the tween decks and coal bunker painting.

We are now in sight of the African coast and can make out several mountains or big hills and some steep sided gorges and it looks a very wild area.

Some excitement today as Chippy has caught himself an eight foot long Blue Shark which has been hanging around under the counter for several hours. Chippy got out the shark hook and baited it with a lump

111

of fatty salt pork and the shark took it straight away. Several of us then dragged it around the ships side until it was abreast of No.3 hatch, got a running bowline over its tail and rove the line through a block and hauled the shark aboard. It was a crazed and savage fish lashing out with its tail and snapping viciously all the time with its jaws. Blomquist rammed an oak capstan bar into its mouth and as far down into its maw as he could and this at least stopped it snapping.

The shark was then treated to the utmost savagery by us in our attempts to kill it. It was clubbed with another capstan bar, attacked with knives and marline spikes and was eventually dispatched by a bullet from the Mates rifle, and a few hefty clouts with a long handled axe.

When it came to the killing of the pigs or the catching of albatross etc. the crew were kindly and did not cause any hurt or harm but with the catching of sharks it was very different and cruelty did often creep in. I have seen some pretty barbaric treatment meted out to sharks that have been landed onto power driven vessels that I have served in and have more than once taken part myself. I suppose it is because sharks are one of a sailors worst enemies.

Chippy opened up the shark but happily we did not find any gruesome remains. He cut off its tail which was presently nailed to the wooden cap in the end of the jib boom. One more trophy to add to the several sharks tails which 'OLIVEBANK' displayed from several of her yard arms.

Chippy then cut out the sharks jaw bones and the teeth, out of which he made a trophy at a later date. He also cut out and cleaned its vertebrae and while this was still soft and pliable he inserted a brass rod through part of its length and shaped it into a walking stick. The shark's skin was as coarse as sandpaper and though the cook did his best to cook some of its flesh, it proved to be very tough and oily and strong tasting and was for the most part unpalatable. Still steering by-the-wind.

Position. 31° 46'S. 30° 11'E.

Sunday 7/5/1939.

Light airs again and not making much headway. We sight land again in the late afternoon out to starboard and as night falls we can see the loom of the lights around and over East London.

Position. 33° S. 28° E.

Course. NW. quarter N.

Monday 8/5/1939.

Breeze is a little fresher today and we make a bit better speed. Most of us are busy 'soogeying' the paintwork. As night falls we can see a lighthouse flashing somewhere in the vicinity of Port Elizabeth.

Position 34° S. 27° E.

Course. N.W. by W.

Tuesday 9/5/1939.

I have developed a type of rash on the right side of my abdomen which has spread over the last 10 days or so and is now the size of a five shilling piece and is now raised up in a rim around its outer edge and the skin inside the rim has started to flake away.

I go and report to the Old Man who makes an examination and then with a very grave expression on his face says "Tell me Townend, when you went to Adelaide, did you see anyone that you liked better than yourself?", which was a very polite way of asking if I had been with some lady of easy virtue. I replied quite truthfully, as was the case, that I had not. Whereupon he informed me that he feared I might have got syphilis.

The Old Man dismissed me but later in the day sent for me and informed me that he had consulted the Medical book and he now thought the rash may be ringworm, so he gave me some crystals of permanganate of potash, told me to dissolve some in water and apply the solution several times a day. Happily for me a few days of this treatment and the problem cleared up, as also the problem of prickly heat had been cleared up on the voyage out. Very useful stuff, permanganate of potash crystals.

Last year (1983) I related this little incident to my son in-law who is a Doctor and he remarked that he had never heard the old man's question phrased so delicately and he felt he might be prompted to use much the same phraseology should the occasion arise.

Position. 35° 28'S 24° 29'E.

Friday 12/5/1939.

We kill another pig.

Saturday 13/5/1939.

This last several days we have been under shortened canvas and steering by-the-wind much of the time. Heavy rain today and a big sea running.

Painting in the tween decks is the job of the day. We pass the Cape of Good Hope at Noon.

Position. 35° S 18° 11'E.

Sunday 14/5/1939.

During the night we see three lighthouses flashing and the loom of light in the sky around Cape Town. At dawn we see the sunrise over Table Mountain, a fine sight to behold.

We appear to be quite close in but are probably 12 or 15 miles distant.

We had a lot of whales around us during the latter part of the night, making a lot of noise as they blew.

During much of the day we have been practically becalmed and have had many albatross swimming around. Chippy who has now got himself the new nick name of "Very morren haps" which is the nearest he can get to "Very good tomorrow perhaps" has caught himself a big one, around nine feet wing tip to wing tip.

Later in the day we had a very heavy rain storm, out of which come a large school of albacore or bonito, hundreds of them, some leaping right out of the water and travelling at a great pace, coming in very close to the ship.

Tonight we can still see the loom of light around Cape Town so we have not progressed very far.

Monday 15/5/1939.

This morning we started once more to bend trade wind sails and get several out of the sail locker for a final check over. The weather mid-morning worsened and came on to blow hard and rain, so we hurriedly stowed away the sails as they were getting too wet.

We took in the royals, topgallants and courses, but by midnight the wind had eased away and we reset everything except upper topgallants and royals.

Wednesday 17/5/1939.

We reset upper topgallants and royals this morning and are now busy chipping rust on the rails and stanchions. Steering 'by-the-wind'.

Thursday 18/5/1939.

Today we have a holiday and sight a steamer in the morning and one again towards evening, both are heading south and are a long way distant.

Arm wrestling seems to be a popular pastime at the moment. I am no good at this for although I am fairly strong, my arms are much too long and offer too much leverage to my opponents.

Friday 19/5/1939.

A good following wind and making better progress. Bending trade wind sails and then chipping rust.

Position 29° 42'S. 14° 20'E.

Course. N. by W half W.

Saturday 20/5/1939.

A steamer sighted us this afternoon which altered course to pass close under our stern. She was a big German tramp named 'ALSTER'. We sight the lights of another vessel about midnight.

Position. 28° 17'S. 11° 55' E. 69.

Sunday 21/5/1939

Hopefully we are heading into better weather. The day men have once more been taken from the watches and now we are only five men and boys to each watch.

Position 27° 14'S. 8° 40'E.

Course N.N.W.

Monday 22/5/1939.

Once more we complete the bending of a lighter suit of sails as we are now once more approaching the tropics. Sails and canvas being expensive, the heavier and newer sails have always to be conserved for the harder weather parts of a voyage and as we are coming home west about, we have had to do much changing of sail, as this way home a vessel usually runs into easier weather. Had we gone east about by way of Cape Horn, 'OLIVEBANK' would no doubt have worn her strongest suit of canvas all the way from Spencer Gulf until she had got into the more temperate zones of the South Atlantic.

Position 25° 7'S 5° 6'E.

Tuesday 23/5/1939,

Once again we are in warmer weather and this day we enter the tropics. Decks are now wet down twice a day, it is first job every morning and last job around sunset. Chipping rust and red leading is the order of the day.

Noon Position. 23° 33'S. 2° 47'E.

Wednesday 24/5/1939.

Trouble today - all hands have to show the soles and heels of their footwear to the mate. It appears that someone has been going around in hobnailed or spiked footwear and has in several places marked the deck. Glad to say I am not guilty both for my own sake and for the 2nd Mates blood pressure. The culprit was never found.

Position 21° 22'S. 0° 49'E.

Thursday 25/5/1939.

Lovely weather. Everyone is now kept busy over-hauling rigging. Artur Blomquist, Olaf Forsten, Lennart Henrikson, and Per Finneman of the starboard watch and Tor Sontag, Artur Berndtson, Alpo Alanen and Unto Kanerva of the port Watch are spending much time working aloft, whilst we others, with less experience, are still chipping away at the rust.

Position 20° S. 0° 50'E.

Friday 26/5/1939.

We sight a sail to starboard this morning and as we close it proves to be 'POMMERN'. She makes a fine sight, as we run together all day.

Pommern from Olivebank 1939

117

Saturday 27/5/1939.

'POMMERN' sails with us again all day but is steadily drawing ahead and is hull down by night fall. Rumour has it that Captain Granith and Captain Broman of 'POMMERN' have a private wager as to which vessel will be first to arrive in the U.K. (I have read of this rumour several times over the past many years but I do not know if there was any substance in it or not).

Position 17° 42'S. 1° 18'W.

Sunday 28/5/1939.

At daybreak we raise St. Helena about 8 miles distant to starboard. It appears to be fairly bleak and barren but rises a fair way out of the water.

Position. 15° 55'S. 5° 42' W.

Monday 29/5/1939. WHITSUNTIDE.

A holiday today. The wind is steady and this is real flying fish weather. There is much activity washing, airing and mending clothes.

Tuesday 30/5/1939.

There's a steady breeze and great weather today. We open all the four hatches and let the air ventilate the tween deck.

The masts and yards are now getting a coat of paint, the standing rigging by now having been coated with Stockholm tar and in some cases with a mixture of melted tallow and white-lead.

Arne Laakso and self are kept occupied chipping rust from the jib boom chain guys. No safety nets beneath us, we just sit on one chain and chip away at the next nearest. Every once in a while we are entertained by bonito playing around the forefoot but we have to watch them with one eye and keep one eye watching that the 2nd Mate doesn't catch us loafing.

Position 13° 15'S. 8° W.

Chipping rust on the jib boom

Wednesday 31/5/1939. to Saturday 3/6/1939.

Steady trade wind and lovely weather. Everywhere there is the smell of fresh paint and linseed oil. Old 'OLIVEBANK' is now being restored to something of her former glory and is looking very smart.

I go to get some water for washing in when we come off watch. This I get from the water tank which is on deck forward, on pulling out my bucket I have two dead rats in it. Someone must have again failed to put on the manhole cover. Not too bad this time as we do not drink the water from this tank but only use it for washing.

Noon Position Saturday 7° 25'S 15° 30'W.

Sunday 4/6/1939.

Steady trade wind and we are steadily making towards home.

Course NNW quarter W. Position 5° 56'S. 16° 49'W.

Monday 5/6/1939.

Lovely weather and a steady breeze. I am once again in disgrace, as I have been greasing sheet and tack wires with fish oil and black grease, using a wad of cotton waste to apply it with, and through my stupidity I let the can tilt and spilt some of the mixture on to our lovely wooden deck up by No.1 hatch.

Once again the 2nd Mate gives me hell and once again he goes the colour of a beetroot.

Presently the Mate comes forward to inspect this vile act of desecration, looks at it, looks at me and says "That Townend, was neither cleverly nor carefully". He then shrugged his shoulders and walked away leaving me to clean up as best I could.

Position 4° 27'S. 19° 9' W.

Tuesday 6/6/1939.

Chipping, red leading, and painting. The lads are now putting the finishing touches to the models they are making, while the weather holds steady. One or two are making sea chest and sea bag handles they finish them off with half hitching and or cross pointing and finally

120

with three, four or even five part Turks heads. The finished object looks quite smart as well as being very useful.

Course N.By.W half W. Position 2° 30'S. 21° 00'W.

Wednesday 7/6/1939.

A light breeze and very hot. 'OLIVEBANK' is not actually becalmed but we are not at the moment making much headway.

Course. N.By W half W. Position.1° 6'S. 23° OO'W.

Thursday 8/6/1939.

We drifted North across the equator about noon today in 24° 00'W.

Friday 9/6/1939.

Lovely hot flying fish weather with many shoals of them about now. Nearly all hands are fully employed with the chipping hammers and red lead at the moment so that almost all of the deck houses and deck fittings look like a patch work quilt.

We see a steamer tonight and signal with the morse lamp. She is bound for South America. In the early morning we sight another one but she is a long way off.

Position. 00 54'N. 25° 30'W.

Sunday 11/6/1939.

Position. 2° 54'N. 28° 16'W.

Monday 12/6/1939.

We have lost the cat. All hands have looked just about everywhere for it but with no success. The 3rd Mate is very upset as he loved the little animal and spent many hundreds of hours playing with it. He thinks someone may have put it overboard. If this is the case and he finds out who has done it, God help the culprit.

Whilst I was at the wheel this forenoon the Old Man took the wheel and told me to go and look over the stern. Very close in, under the counter was a big shark probably about 14 feet in length.

Chippy baited the shark hook with salt pork but evidently the shark didn't fancy it and he swam a little way off. Presently it came back and was swimming alongside the ship. Artur Blomquist threw it an empty seven pound margarine tin which it immediately swallowed.

Artur Berndtson then conjured up an iron bar, attached a piece of line to it and tried several times to harpoon the shark but with no success and presently it sheers off.

During the afternoon we have a lot of bonito swimming with us and the 3rd Mate catches one though he manages to cover himself in blood when he kills it. They are fine to eat and have the colour and texture of pork or veal and make a welcome change from our usual diet. Presently a shark appears and frightens the school of bonito away.

Towards evening a large school of albacore springing high out of the water come charging down on us, we try our hand at the fishing lines but we are out of luck.

Course. N.by E. three quarters E.

Position. 4° 38'N. 25° 32'W.

Tuesday 13/6/1939.

Today we have the doldrums once more and so we spend much of the watch at the braces, trying to trim the yards round, first this way and then that way in the hopes of trying to catch every last puff of wind.

We are now in the South American shipping lane and during the day we sight six steam and motor driven vessels, three of which come close in. First we have Lamport & Holts, "CRISPIN" of Liverpool, then a Norwegian "ROSE" and lastly a German "PETROPOLIS". This is a big event for us, sighting 6 vessels in one day.

Once again we try to catch a shark but have no luck.

The noon position today is 11 miles nearer to the equator than at noon yesterday. There has been so little wind that we must have been drifting in a Southerly direction.

Wednesday 14/6/1939.

Doldrums and becalmed all through the night and then at 0615 hours this morning we experience a very strong and sudden rain squall which takes everyone by surprise and in a matter of seconds it is snowing canvas again.

We lose, in rapid succession, the outer jib, fore lower and upper topsails and royal, and the mizzen upper topsail.

Plenty of 'hurry up' for all hands getting in the remnants of these light fair weather rags but I fear that for the most part they are too far gone to be repaired. Both watches work until late afternoon, sending down the remnants and bending new sails.

Thursday 15/6/1939.

It would appear that we have picked up the North East trades in quick time, as we have a fairly strong steady breeze today. This morning we have bent 3 topgallant staysails.

We try to hook some more bonito but no luck today with this project.

Friday 16/6/1939.

Lovely weather with plenty of flying fish so painting and cleaning is the order of the day.

We bend a flying jib and steer by the wind all day.

Position. 9° 6'N. 32°W.

Saturday 17/6/1939.

Steady trade wind speeding us nicely towards home. Much washing and drying of clothes and blankets and airing of blankets and donkeys breakfasts. Steering full and by the wind.

Position. 11° 23'N. 33° 42'W.

Sunday 18/6/1939.

Steering full and by the wind.

Position. 14° 30'N. 33° 42'W.

Monday 19/6/1939.

The trade wind is holding steady and we are making 8 to 9 knots. We are still a long way from home but it makes us think that the Liverpool girls have already got hold of the tow rope.

Liverpool girls have a hold of the tow rope

Started to paint the deck houses with white paint today and by knocking off time much of the patchwork of red lead has been covered over and things are looking much better. We sighted a vessel heading south during the night but she was a long way off.

Chippy has somehow preserved a flying fish which he has mounted on a stand with its wings outstretched, and he has given it a coat of varnish and the finished article looks really good. I have been having a good yarn with him in his cabin and he has been showing me the receipts for the fines he had to pay to the powers that be in Maitland. All together it has cost him 1005 Finmarks - equivalent to around £4.55 in todays currency and would no doubt be well in excess of one month's hard earned pay.

The list of offences were as follows:-

I/ Drunkenness.

2/ Damage to a sanitary pail.

3/ Common Assault (2 charges).

4/ Disorderly conduct.

Under shipboard conditions he was a quiet enough chap and in no way a trouble maker but like many more of his kind, which includes me, a smell of the barmaids or barmans apron after long weeks at sea would often tend to cause a truly law abiding seafarer to do silly things.

Position. 17° 42'N. 37° 14'W.

Tuesday 20/6/1939.

Trade winds still holding fair and old 'OLIVEBANK' is making good progress.

I caused the Old Man and myself some concern this morning, just after turning to time.

While standing on the starboard pin rail abreast of No.4 hatch drawing up buckets of sea water for wetting down the decks, I under estimated the speed we were travelling and the consequent drag on the bucket when it hit the water and I was nearly taken overboard.

The Old Man was on the poop and on seeing me quickly disappear from his view he rushed to the break of the poop to see if I was still aboard.

Finding out that I was still aboard he gave me a well deserved bawling out for being so bloody stupid and then three lessons in, how and how not, to get water from over the side of a fast moving vessel. Finally he gave me the cheerful message that if I had gone overboard, there was no way they could have stopped 'OLIVEBANK' in time to get me. Probably a shark would have had me anyway.

Position 20° 46'N. 35° 32'W.

Wednesday 21/6/1939.

Steady trade wind, we have hardly touched the braces this past several days, apart from taking a pull on them just to freshen the nip before the end of each watch.

This is real bosuns' weather and the paint is now getting slapped on by most of us under the very watchful eyes of the mates and several harsh words in our ears if we leave any 'holidays'.

Blomquist spends much of today suspended in a bosuns chair re-painting our lovely figurehead "OLIVE". He does a really fine artistic job, black tresses, lovely pink cheeks and blue and white flowing robes.

Position. 23° 12'N. 39° 57'W.

Thursday 22/6/1939.

Weather, wind and work, just as yesterday.

Course. N.by E. three quarters E. Position. 24° 28'N. 40° 22'W.

Friday 23/6/1939.

During the night the wind fades away and we only have very light airs all day. All hands finish work at 1500 hours as a special concession, as tomorrow is a holiday.

Course. NNE. half E. Position. 25° 36'N. 40° 06'W.

Saturday 24/6/1939. MIDSUMMER DAY.

It is a holiday for all hands. The Old Man has had all the day men up on the poop and he has been showing them how to use a sextant. Whilst I was at the wheel there was much merriment over this business, as Chippy managed to get his beard fouled up in the sextant. All those concerned were shown something of the intricacies of navigation and a good time was enjoyed by all.

Course. NNW.

Position. 27° 03'N. 39° 32'W.

Sunday 25/6/1939.

We have little wind all day and roll around quite a lot in an oily swell. This rolling and lack of wind causes much slatting and banging of the sails, and creaking and groaning of the rigging and at times the various noises aloft get quite deafening.

The sun beats down and it is very hot. We get a light breeze by early evening and brace round onto the port tack.

Monday 26/6/1939.

A light breeze, holding a steady course with the lower yards braced hard onto the backstays. I had been aloft overhauling buntlines early this morning and as I descended the lower rigging I did some sort of damn fool trapeze act and was rewarded for my pains with a 12 to 15 foot fall onto the hard deck. The 2nd Mate rushed up to see if I was still breathing. On finding out I had only suffered a bit of a shaking and a sprained wrist (both well deserved), he said he was glad to note that I had landed on deck with my shoulder and arm taking the strain and bearing the brunt of the fall, for had I landed on my head I should have put some unsightly dents in the new deck planking and thus buggered up its general appearance.

Course. N. by E. three quarters E.

Position. 28° 06'N. 39° 32'W.

Wednesday 28/6/1939.

Very little wind but have managed to wear ship and are now on starboard tack and steering by the wind.

The Italian steamer 'ROCCA' passes quite close to us about 0830 this morning. She is flying her ensign at half mast so we presume someone on board has died.

It would appear my old mate Chippy does not like the Italians very much. Normally he is a quiet peace loving man - at least when we are at sea. He sprang up into the lower rigging gesticulating wildly and shaking his fist at the 'ROCCA' and shattering the peace by hurling insults in his native tongue at those aboard her. Finally in the best English invective that he could muster, still shaking his fist he informed them that, "Fokking Musoolini is a fokking, blerry barstan" the last two words being the nearest he ever did get to "bloody bastard". I was glad to note I had at least one Shipmate who shared my sentiments regarding this little fat, loud-mouthed consumer of macaroni.

Thursday 29/6/1939.

Most of the painting both aloft and around the deck has now been finished apart from a few final touches.

This morning we are under the fo'c'sle head scraping away at the old paintwork and touching up the bare patches with red lead. A lot of old paint and scale has to be removed from the deck head and this is a bit of a strain on the neck and shoulders. Mostly we are standing on boxes etc to make it easier to reach up but big Sam Johansson a young, quiet, softly spoken giant of a lad, is just able to reach up to do his patch of work whilst having his feet still firmly planted on the deck. Sam is a really powerful lad and though he does not say much is a good shipmate and a good watch mate and when he tails onto a haliard or starts to tramp round the capstan, he makes his presence felt.

Course. N.by.E. three quarters E.

Position. 30° 39'N. 39° 43'W.

128

Friday 30/6/1939.

There is a moderate breeze with lovely weather and we are now back at work changing the remaining light weather sails for the heavier canvas. Although it is summer time in the Northern hemisphere we can still get some heavy weather before we reach the U.K.

The last several days we have had patches of Sargasso or Gulf Weed drifting around - some of these masses of weed being quite extensive in area and measuring many square yards.

We also have many Portuguese men of war drifting around. These sea creatures are a type of jelly fish with what looks like an inflated air bag protruding above the surface of the water which acts as a sail and when the wind gets up they travel through the water at a very fast pace. They are known by sailing ship men as, "By the wind jelly fish".

We sight one steamer today, heading for America.

Saturday 1/7/39.

We complete the sail changing today and this should be the last time for this task on this voyage.

Two more vessels passed us in the early morning hours, as we are now getting into the shipping lanes between the Mediterranean Sea and the U.S.A.

Today, Chippy killed another pig, so now we have fresh meat in plenty.

Course. N.E.half N.

Position. 34° 15'N. 39° 42'W.

Sunday 2/7/39.

Little wind again this day and only slow progress. Two of the daymen have now been returned to each watch, which helps things along a little, as now we shall take less tricks at the wheel and spend less time on look-out duty.

A big shark has been swimming around today, coming right up to the surface and close in to the ships' side. We make repeated attempts to catch it, both with shark hook and harpoon but we do not have any luck.

Monday 3/7/1939.

Steady breeze and beautiful weather. Nearly all hands are now employed with the task of scraping the bright work, teak rails, cabin skylights, chartroom, poop and fo'c'sle doors etc. in fact everything that is made of hardwood. We sight two tankers one British named 'LAUREL WOOD' passes close under our stern with a dip of the ensign and a few blasts on her siren.

Course. N.E.quarter E.

I have lookout tonight from 22.00 to 23.00 hours. It is a beautiful moonlit night and moonlight over the sea can play queer tricks with the imagination.

I sensed a tingling of the spine and on looking around and about for a probable reason, I saw someone laying out on the foreyard, but could not make out who it was. Almost immediately the person or vision disappeared. I waited for the thud as someone hit the deck, or the splash as someone hit the sea, but happily I did not hear either.

When I was relieved of my lookout duty I made enquiries as to which of the watch had been sent up onto the foreyard, but it seems that no-one had been up there.

I pursued this next day with all the lads of the Port watch, thinking possibly that a practical joke had been played, but all of the port watch assured me that none of them had been aloft and eventually the only explanation that could be offered was that on the very odd occasion similar sightings had been made, but not always necessarily from the foreyard. It was said that it was the ghost (if that is the correct term) of a poor unfortunate lad who fell from aloft and was killed some years previously and who appeared from time to time.

I don't know how many lads were unfortunate and unlucky enough to have fallen from the rigging of the 'OLIVEBANK' and been killed but I feel there must have been several in her lifetime of over 46 years of sailing the oceans. I do know of one young lad named Tyler who met his death in this manner in 1927, however.

The whole incident may have been supposition on my part, it may have been caused by a combination of moonlight, shadow, the eerie creaking and groaning of cordage, coupled to the rather vivid imagination of a young and to some degree superstitious sailor. But, see something I am sure I did and even now 45 years later I can still, in my mind's eye, see someone on that foreyard.

I was, as a young lad brought up, more or less in the fishing community at Bridlington East Yorkshire where in those days many superstitions were rife, especially amongst the elder members of the community and some of it probably rubbed off onto me but I assure anyone who may read this, that I am serious about the incident and in no way trying to pull anyone's leg.

Tuesday 4/7/39.

Very little wind this morning and we are more or less becalmed. We spend much of today at the braces trimming the yards from port to starboard and starboard to port, trying to catch every puff of wind.

It is very hot and everyone gets a bit foul tempered and consequently much foul language (of the international variety) is being hurled around. In between the 'pulley-hauley' sessions we return to the task of scraping the bright work which gets a bit tedious but is a far better task to perform than using prayer books on the deck planking.

We have a shark hanging around again but he isn't interested in our fatty pork and won't take the hook.

Many small jelly fish abound and also many small birds much like swallows flying around.

The British steamer 'PATIO' of Liverpool passed close astern of us today.

Position. 36° 08'N. 38°14' W._

Wednesday 5/7/39.

This morning we have got a nice following wind and are making good progress towards 'Merree' England.

The 2nd Mate catches me whistling and plays hell a bit. He says I will drive the wind away, which is another superstition among sailing ship men. He says if I wanted to whistle I should have done it yesterday when we were becalmed, for it might have had the effect of whistling up some wind for us.

Tasks for today - scraping teak and scrubbing the deck using a solution of soda water and a sprinkling of sand. This job was often known as barbarizing.

We sight 3 more steamers today but all are a long way off.

Course. N.N.E.half E.

Thursday 6/7/39.

A strong breeze today with a big sea and we are taking plenty of water on deck. The ship is really bowling along and making 10 knots. At noon we are abreast of the Azores which probably explains the presence of all the small birds of two days ago.

We are this day kept in full employment scraping the deck head under the foc'sle head as there is too much water swilling around the deck to do anything out there. Both galley doors are shut tight, with much rattling of the cooking utensils and of course many loud oaths emanating from within. Though he is working under great difficulty the cook will surely conjure up something reasonably good for us to eat.

Looking back over the years it seems a trifle sad that we only complained when things went wrong and never congratulated him when he made superhuman efforts to get us something hot to eat and drink. "If you can read this Rolf, from your place up aloft, please accept my heartfelt thanks and my apologies for all the uncalled for hard words of which you were so often the recipient and which for the most part you bore with a grin, for not many times did I see you get upset by your fellow men." We sight one steamer.

Course. ENE quarter E. Position. 39°30' N. 37°00' W.

Friday 7/7/39.

Wind and sea have both eased away considerably, and we are once more scrubbing away at the deck - happily with brooms and not with

132

short hand brushes. We are all stripped to the waist as it is hot work under the blazing sun.

Presently we get soaked, caused by a torrential downpour of rain but carry on with the scrubbing. The old man came out on deck after the rain had stopped and seeing our wet and gleaming pelts, straight away stops the job and sends us all to get dried and to change our gear, saying if we don't we shall surely all finish up with rheumatism.

Such was Captain Graniths' consideration for his men. Since the time of these events it has been my great good fortune to have served under several fine British Master Mariners on long voyages and short ones but seldom did I experience the consideration accorded to us by Captain Granith. He was a real old "sea daddy" to us lads and for my part, on reflection, was not only well respected but also much loved, if one is permitted to use such an expression.

Course. ESE.half E. Position. 41° 40'N. 33° 25'W.

Saturday 8/7/39.

Moderate breeze but very variable and so once again we spend most of our time during the watch, at the braces trimming the yards to catch the maximum amount of wind.

All the months of sweating and straining on brace, clew line, and halliard have toughened us up no end and mostly we are developing some fair muscles and chests and we don't have to try and convey the image that we are tough, for tough we are indeed.

We experience several heavy rain squalls and spread canvas in which we catch much water with which to top up the forward tanks which by now are at a very low level.

Sunday 9/7/39.

The wind was still variable most of the morning and so we were steering by the wind, with the yards screw braced but by mid-afternoon the wind has shifted round and we are braced up square running before a following wind.

A lovely sunny day and all hands busy washing clothes now that we have plenty of fresh water.

Blomquist spots a very large turtle swimming by.

Position. 43°35'N. 30°26'W.

Monday 10/7/39.

A steady following breeze today and the tasks are, oiling all the deck planking, coating the scuppers with bitumen and cutting in and painting the bottom eighteen inches or so of all the deck houses with brown paint.

The lower section of each deck house had not been painted until we had completed the deck scrubbing so as to avoid scarring with the caustic soda.

The paint was very thick and more like glue than paint, it being the Mates very own concoction. It was made up of several odd lots of paints and scrapings from a score of paint pots all mixed up together in a drum and boiled up on the blacksmiths hearth. The Mate and 3rd Mate did the boiling up and stirring and all went well until the bloody lot caught fire and then there was a commotion to be sure. The fire was soon extinguished however with little damage or mess.

Linseed oil was then added to the contents of the drum and stirred well in and then it was doled out to us lads in tins then, armed each with a brush, we went to work but not before being told by the Mate that there would be a rewarding kick aimed at the backside of any son of a gun who left any holidays. This was given with a merry twinkle in his eye, a huge grin and a flash of his gold fillings.

A large American oil tanker passes us today and we sight another steamer towards night fall.

Course. E.by.S.

Position. 44° 35' N. 28° 53' W.

Tuesday 11/7/39.

A steady breeze and lovely weather and the old ship is bringing us nearer home as each day passes.

We have bonito under the forefoot leaping high out of the water at times. In our free time Laakso and I crouch down in the knight heads and proceed to fish. We soon hooked a big one and managed to land it into the knight heads where it kicked and struggled no end. The only thing to do was kill it or we might lose it overboard again, so we killed it with a knife but not without a struggle and by the time it was dead we were both covered in fish slime and blood.

This in itself did not matter but what did matter was the fact that the Mates freshly painted knight heads, only completed a few days before, were badly defiled with blood, slime and fish guts and before we had time to clean things up he decided to take a walk up for'ard which proved not to be too good for his blood pressure.

On seeing all the mess and carnage spread around he gave us both a terrible bawling out and of course we had to clean up all the mess, which was fair enough but I couldn't help thinking to myself, "I don't know what the hell he is griping at, after all, he will get his fair share of fresh fish for his tea."

A few short years later when I was a young and I hope, conscientious bosun serving in Prince Lines 'SICILIAN PRINCE' on what turned out to be a voyage of 2 years and 10 days duration under wartime conditions. There was a shortage of paint and almost everything else and then I could see the wisdom of Ragnar's thoughts and could fully understand his rage, for to most 1st Mates and many bosuns, paintwork becomes something of an obsession.

I have to admit that in more than one impoverished old tramp ship I have boiled up all the pot bottoms and scraping to make things eke out - yes - I've had the bloody lot on fire as well.

Position. 45° 15'N. 27° 36'W.

Wednesday 12/7/39.

There is a strong breeze and the old ship is rolling a bit. She seems a bit heavy on the wheel today as she appears to have been for this past several days but its roll and go now and we are not very far from home and a good pint or two or three or four or more. The donkey boiler is now completely overhauled and is ready for use when the need arises.

We make the first preparations for a landfall today as the first job is to unplug both hawse pipes, lead the chain cables through them and up to the anchors which are still lashed and stowed on the fo'c'sle head and each cable is then shackled up to its anchor.

Position. 46° 50'N. 24° 05'W.

Anchors still lashed on fo'c'sle head

Friday 14/7/39.

There has been a very strong wind today, all day. The Liverpool girls have now surely got hold of the tow rope, for we are now bowling along making a steady 9 knots. The starboard watch took in all 3 Royals at 1600 hours.

The British steamer 'CORDILLERIA' passed us today. 'OLIVEBANK' must have made a fine sight to those aboard her as she charged along under full sail and with a big bone in her teeth. Port watch took in the cro'jack all three upper top gallants and several staysails in their watch before midnight as the wind freshened up a lot.

Course. E.S.E.

*Position. 48° 34'N. 19° 35*W.*

In my scrap log I have spelt 'CORDILLEREA' thus, but feel that this was a mistake. 'CORDILLERIA' was to the best of my knowledge owned by Donaldson Line of Glasgow and was a freezer ship used chiefly in the South American meat trade. Little was I to know on that day in 1939, that she was to be the last vessel in which I was ever to serve, when under her new name of 'BRANSFIELD' and flying the house flag of United Whalers (Hector Whaling) I went south in her to the Antarctic Ice for the 1952/1953 whaling season where she was employed as attendant freezer ship to the 'BALAENA EXPEDITION'. This job of work she had carried out for several years prior to 1952 and continued to do for several years more until she was superseded by a larger vessel named 'ENDERBY'. The last time I was aboard 'BRANSFIELD' would be in June 1957 when she was undergoing a refit for the coming whaling season at Tonsberg in Norway.

Saturday 15/7/39.

A very strong wind and big seas, probably the heaviest seas of the voyage, are crashing aboard. The figure head and knight heads are burying themselves in the ocean, and as the old vessel lifts she is scooping up green water over the fo's'cle head and rolling both rails under and we are getting much water on deck.

When we came on watch at midnight we were soon aloft taking in all three lower to'gallants and the main upper topsail which, with a loud crack, had rent asunder and was whipping about like a thing possessed. This took us a little time to get stowed.

137

During the 0800 to 1300 watch the weather eased a little and we of the starboard watch sent down the remains of the main upper topsail. Then we bent a new sail in its place and set it.

The wind eases off a bit in mid afternoon and Chippy and Arno Stromberg the steward manage to kill and dress the last of the pigs but it was a difficult enough job to do with the old ship pitching and rolling as she was doing and still taking a fair amount of water on deck from time to time.

The 2nd Mate has told me that at noon today 15/7/39 we are 210 miles to the nearest point of Ireland, 280 miles to Queenstown, 380 miles to Falmouth.

Course. E.S.E.

Position. 49° 37'N. 14° 36'W.

Sunday 16/7/39.

Wind and sea have both eased off a bit but the sea is still running high. We of the starboard watch have set lower to'gallants during the 0400 to 0800 watch.

There are many sea birds with us now, which is a most welcome sight, as we must now be nearing land.

The old man has sighted some vessel ahead of us and we get the order to set the spanker and outer jib. We presently overtake the vessel which turns out to be a steam trawler with her mizzen sail set. She is making very heavy weather of it and nearly standing on end. I bet her poor cook is having a hell of a time, especially with his galley situated so near the stern.

When the watch was relieved at 0800 my old watch mate and cabin mate Arne Laakso and self ate breakfast together. I think he must have had a bad attack of Channel Fever (The Channels) as through breakfast he acted very oddly, grinning in a most stupid manner and gibbering away like an ape. As soon as he had eaten his fill he got out his sheath knife and started to prod me in the ribs with it - not drawing any blood - but just pricking me and all the time still grinning and gibbering. When I asked him what he thought he was playing at I just got another prick in the rib for an answer, so I got off the wooden bench on which we were both sitting, and fetched him a quick crisp clout on his jaw, which knocked him clean off the bench and he finished up on his backside away in the corner of our fo'c'sle.

It seemed to have the desired effect for he sheathed his knife pretty quickly and wiped the grin off his face and never uttered another sound.

This afternoon the starboard watch set the main upper to'gallant and in the 1900 to 2400 watch the port watch clear both anchors over the side, so that they are both ready for letting go. We sight a steamer towards night fall.

Landfall at last, we pick up the Fastnet light before midnight and the port watch set the fore and mizzen upper top gallants, main royal and all the remaining staysails.

Steering by the wind.

Course. NE.by.E.quarter E.

Monday 17/7/39.

We sight several vessels during the watch from midnight to 0400 and at day break we are well in sight of the Irish Coast and are travelling steadily up towards Queenstown.

There is very little wind and a calm sea. We are fairly close in and can clearly see the cliffs, villages and lighthouses and with the breeze coming off the land we can smell the very pleasant fragrance of the truly rural and beautiful countryside.

It is indeed a pleasure and a joy to see all the expanse of lush greenery, for this is the first time we have sighted green pastures since we sailed from Donaghadee last October. Any land we have seen since that time has either been brown sunbaked, or barren, with the exception of the parks and gardens of Adelaide.

Now I know why they call this fair land the Emerald Isle.

Slowly now, we are approaching a light vessel and are in company with several small fishing vessels.

Presently we come up to the Daunt Lightship and pick the pilot up close by and soon we can see Queenstown and some of its shipping.

Now we have plenty of work and plenty 'hurry up' as we start to take in sail, the Royals first, then to'gallants and courses and finally some of the staysails. We don't go inside the harbour but anchor outside at 1930.

Olivebank at anchor. Queenstown 17/7/1939

The anchor goes down with a big splash and a roar of the cable, a pleasant sound after 119 days at sea.

We are laying about two and a half miles from the shore and about one mile from Queenstown itself. The Customs boat comes alongside and Customs Officers come aboard. I don't think they will find any contraband aboard old 'OLIVEBANK' for had we had any it would long since have been eaten, drunk or smoked.

Several small boats with curious sightseers are sailing all around us, their occupants taking photos and chatting to us and asking us all the usual questions.

We have all the sails and gear snugged down by 2015 hours and by this time several of the people have been allowed aboard to look around.

When all the visitors have departed we start with the celebrations as both the Captain and the Mate give us some rum which goes down very well indeed.

This is followed by a concoction that some of the lads had been making some couple of months previously rather secretly. It was simply yeast, sugar, raisins and water, which had been mixed up and allowed to stand in two 5 gallon kerosene drums which I think would probably have had a bit of a swill out with a drop of water prior to putting in the ingredients.

It tasted lovely, especially diluted with a little water but it did not seem to mix too well with the rum and soon it was noticeable that some of the lads were turning a funny greyish green colour and having to dash out on deck.

I smoked two cigarettes, the first for four months and presently it came my turn to make a quick dash outside.

There seemed to be a bit of a commotion going on outside. The Mate was on top of our cabin and he was remonstrating with big Unto Kanerva about something or other to do with the standard compass which was situated there, when amidst a lot of shouting the Mate came hurtling down onto the deck. Whether he fell, or whether he was pushed, I do not know, as it was by this time dark and I wasn't seeing too clearly anyway. Luckily the Mate picked himself up and did not seem any the worse for having hurtled to the deck.

The party no doubt went on until all the drink was expended but by now I for one was out of the running and glad to crawl into my bunk.

The name for the booze that the lads made was KILJU pronounced KILL YOO - and it nearly did just that.

Tuesday 18/7/39.

Those of us who were able, mustered on deck at "turn to" time but the ranks were sadly depleted, nobody felt like work and nobody was really capable of work. The second mate who was in charge didn't seem too good either, he surveyed us with a somewhat jaundiced eye and then surveyed the very much defiled deck and we were ordered to get buckets and brooms and clean up all the mess that had been made. This job took some little while but when it was completed to his entire satisfaction at Midday he told us that it had been a 'job and finish' and that we were free for the rest of the day, much to our delight.

In the afternoon the American liner 'WASHINGTON' came in to land passengers from New York but she is soon away again.

Our passenger leaves us today and as he had only condescended to speak about a dozen words all voyage, begrudgingly at that, I didn't offer to help him to get his gear down into the boat. As he was departing Chippy, who was still in his cups caused a laugh. He walked up to the passenger with a very grave expression on his face and in perfect English, loud and clear simply said "Excuse me Hong Kong," which to all of us at that time seemed most amusing. Those four words were all that he said and none of us were ever to learn what the message really was.

Wednesday 19/7/39.

All hands over the side on stages today chipping and scraping at the rust patches and scars and touching up with red lead. Lovely weather and a pleasant enough job as we can watch the movement of the shipping and call out to the parties who come out in small craft to get a closer look at 'OLIVEBANK' and also as an added bonus one could have a crafty drag on a fag as long as none of the Mates saw you.

I recall that we were in sight of a very large Church which had a carillon and the tuneful peel of those bells sounded really beautiful as it came across the water and could be heard very clearly.

A young lady passenger arrives today. It is Miss Isabella Kiernander who is a great lover of sailing vessels and who later had an excellent book of sea poems published entitled, "Songs of the Tall Ships", with drawings by C. Wylie and several photographs of some of the latter day square riggers. It is a book of only 60 pages but is well worth having as Miss Kiernander had a great understanding of ships and sailormen which becomes very evident as one reads through its pages.

The book was published by Alexander Moring Ltd., The De la More Press, 2A Cook St., Bond St. W.I. I fear it may be very hard to obtain a copy these days, as it was published early during the war but to anyone who may be sufficiently interested it is well worth while obtaining, should the opportunity arise.

Olivebank waiting for orders anchored off Queenstown 1939

I feel it is worthy of note to write the following lines with which this little book is dedicated.

DEDICATION

To Douglas William Stewart who first taught me to love the tall ships of 'Mariehamn'.

To Captain Carl Granith who showed me their beauty;

To Geoffrey Robertshaw who keeps them in his heart; and to the windjammers we have loved together ~ those that have passed and those that still remain.

To all who sail the great waters and those, who rest beneath the seas.

To a memory of London river, and the Finnish Four Masted Barque

'PONAPE'.

The first poem of 11 verses is entitled 'The Ship Lover' and is dedicated to the Finnish Four Masted Barque 'OLIVEBANK'.

Thursday 20/7/39.

The old man receives the orders this morning - we are to go to Barry Dock to discharge.

Shortly after noon we man the Capstan and commence the long hard task of weighing anchor, once again by the 'Armstrong Patent method' (as coal is too expensive). We didn't have a Shanty man as shanties did not seem to be used in these last days of sail but we joyfully tramped the Capstan, all the time gleefully singing out "Sist Gong, Sist Gong" which means "Last time", how bloody mistaken we proved to be.

All the time we were weighing anchor and making sail we had a playful whale swimming around us, probably in its own way, bidding a farewell to we toilers of the deep.

We have a steady following wind which takes us over to the entrance of the Bristol Channel and we sight many vessels on our passage over. These were the great days of the South Wales coal trade and of all those hard case old tramps which used to convey it to all ports of the world and of the coastwise and continental colliers which in those times could be seen most anywhere and everywhere. Sadly now for the most part, those old vessels and the breed of men who sailed them have, like the coal trade, just about disappeared.

Friday 21/7/39.

'OLIVEBANK' makes a steady passage over and we raise Lundy Island about 1830 hours. Many vessels around all day which include several steam trawlers at their fishing. Jobs for the passage over are just the routine jobs of cleaning the ship and the brass work and the last odd touch of paint here and there.

'OLIVEBANK' is now really spick and span. It is said that beauty is in the eye of the beholder but beautiful she looked to us and beautiful she must have looked to those in the ships that passed by, for majestic and beautiful she was indeed. Though, like all of her kind, she could on occasion be a bitch and both kill and maim, just as all vessels right down the centuries have and no doubt still do to this day.

My old watch mate Arne Laakso and self are still the best of pals I am happy to say and no mention has been made by either of us about the odd incident of a few days ago.

We got news whilst in Queenstown that Hitler and his mob of gangsters appear to be shouting the odds a bit and it looks as if a war is in the offing.

Saturday 22/7/39.

The old ship is now nearing the end of another long voyage, as we head steadily up the Bristol Channel with the North Devon and Somerset coasts to starboard and the coast of Glamorgan to port.

Very many vessels of several types are travelling this water way but mostly tramps, coasters and trawlers.

We pick up the Pilot about 1000 hrs and proceed into Barry roads where we arrive at noon and once again anchor and wait for the tide.

During the afternoon I take Miss Kiernander on a tour of the ship and at her request and with the permission of the several crew members, I escort her into both fo'c'sles, which appeared to be of much interest to her. As we emerged from our small deck house I was slightly amused to see that the first and second Mates were both hovering in very close proximity to our fo'c'sle wearing rather anxious expressions. They had no need to worry. Miss Kiernander was in safe hands.

The day was cold and wet in the morning but faired up nicely in the afternoon.

At about 1945 hrs we heard three blasts on the Mate's whistle and we all tumbled out on deck and started, for what surely was the last time, to tramp round the fo'c'sle head straining on a Capstan bar, breaking the anchor out of Bristol Channel mud. The two tugs arrived at 2000 hrs and took us into and through the lock. There were many interested people standing on the lock side asking all manner of questions. Then we moved up the dock where we came alongside and made fast abreast of Rank's flour mill.

Olivebank in Barry Docks 1939

Everything being snugged down by 2330 hrs our voyage was now over 'OLIVEBANK' had completed another grain race.

Mr. Anderson the 2nd Mate told me that 'OLIVEBANK' had covered a distance of 28,000 miles on this voyage.

How many times we tacked and wore ship, how many times we gave a swing on the braces or a long heave on some halliard or other I know not but the callouses on the palms of our hands were sufficient evidence that we had executed these duties many, many times. Not only were our hands hard but we, this happy little band of youngish men and boys, were all of us toughened and physically hard.

'OLIVEBANK' had brought her crew and cargo of 4,400 tons of wheat halfway round the world and in my case, safely home.

The 1939 freight rates were poor indeed. I was told they were around £1.5.0 shillings - £l-25p per ton.

Sunday 23/7/39.

Today we said farewell to our lady passenger - Miss Kiernander as she left the ship for her home in Worthing.

Later in the day Captain Granith sent for me and asked when I required to be paid off and as it was my hope and intention to make another round voyage in the old vessel (subject of course to the Captains approval), I asked if I could remain on articles for a week or two in the hope that the situation in Europe may ease somewhat, to which he kindly agreed.

'OLIVEBANK' was due to go home to Mariehamn for a general refit after she had discharged the cargo and I felt that it might not be a very good idea for me, a lone Englishman to risk getting bottled up in the Baltic if hostilities were to break out.

Our stay in Barry dock was pleasant enough, many people came to visit the ship and much interest and pleasure was shown by the general public as a whole.

Thomson Street in those days was typical of most sea ports, where the shops purveyed all manner of goods, which attracted the eyes of seafarers. It was also fairly cosmopolitan and did, I believe, provide other dubious delights in some of its establishments.

I passed through Barry several years ago now and mostly the old order of things had disappeared and as I recall some of the buildings had been demolished.

Four little things stand out in my mind regarding our stay in that busy, at that time, South Wales Port.

1. A catchy tune called 'South of the Border' was all the rage on the radio, and even to this day it reminds me of 'OLIVEBANK' and Barry Dock whenever I hear it.

2. There was a hospital down by the coast not far from our berth and several of the young nurses used to come down to visit the ship on these summer evenings. The old man kindly gave permission for them to come aboard and look over the ship, and they were even allowed to come into our fo'c'sle to chat. Two conditions had to be strictly adhered to, one being, that while the girls were in the fo'c'sle the doors had at all times to be left wide open and two, they had to be off the ship and give

themselves plenty of time to get back to the hospital before dark.

3. The good people connected with the Scandinavian Seamans' Church in Cardiff visited us and arranged several coach outings, which were most enjoyable. All the more so because several of the girls who attended the church were present on these trips, which usually took the form of a coach outing and picnic. Two of the girls I recall, one Finnish and I think the Pastor's daughter and the other being from one of the Baltic States, I think Latvia, her father was himself a seaman.

4. The fourth incident being one which caused us much mirth, namely the unshipping of the swing doors at the Cadoxton Working Mens Club. The committee and members of this club which was up at the top end of the dock, had very kindly extended a warm welcome to all of us aboard 'OLIVEBANK' and were goodness itself when any of us entered through its portals.

After we had been in Barry several days we were confronted by a very wrathful 2nd Mate as we mustered at turning to time one morning. He told us that a complaint had been received from the club that the swing doors had been unshipped (but I think not damaged) by someone of 'OLIVEBANK's' complement. He gave us hell and went on at great length and told us that the culprit or culprits should be thoroughly ashamed of themselves and that they must go that very evening and apologise and endeavour to make amends (all this being fair enough comment).

As we set about our daily tasks and talked a little about this latest incident we realized that none of the P.O.'s or the fo'c'sle crowd were involved, which whittled things down a bit.

On mustering again after dinner, we were once again confronted by a somewhat sheepish 2nd Mate who was big enough to make an apology to us, for as he said, bawling us out, as he now knew that none of us had been involved.

We later discovered that it was our 1st Mate Ragnar who had perpetrated this terrible offence.

During my stay in Barry the time was pleasantly spent. It was summer time with long light evenings when we strolled to Barry Island to the fun fair, or walked down to the coast and watched the many ships passing

148

up and down the Bristol Channel.

During the two weeks that I stayed, we first of all gave the old ship a good harbour stow when all the yards were neatly and symmetrically brought into line which gave her a very tidy appearance aloft.

Most of the crew spent much of the working day over the side on stages, chipping and scraping away the rust scars of a 14,000 mile voyage and patching up the scars with red lead and then black paint.

After several days laid alongside it would seem that a lengthy stay in port was envisaged, as 'OLIVEBANK' had not yet started to discharge her cargo. So it was decided to send down and stow at least some of the sails, which we commenced to do.

As the days progressed it became very apparent that the situation in Europe was not going to ease and therefore I very reluctantly decided that it would probably be wiser for me to pay off and go home.

Albin Bjorkman had expressed a wish to sail with me in a British ship if this was possible, so we both approached Captain Granith concerning this matter. The Captain doubted very much that Albin would be allowed to serve in a British vessel signing articles in a British Port but readily agreed to arrange to pay Albin off if he could get a berth in one. As I recall the Captain allowed us some time off next day to pursue this matter, so off we went to make the necessary enquiries, paying a visit to the Board of Trade, Shipping Federation and National Union of Seamen offices, where we learned that it was not possible for Albin to become employed in the British Mercantile Marine. (A few short months later when our ships and seamen were getting the hell belted out of them by U-Boats and surface raiders, I feel that Albin's services may quite well have been much sought after.) We came back aboard and made our report to the old man and at this time I arranged to be paid off on August 5th.

Paying off day duly arrived and I was heralded into the saloon where the Captain spoke kindly to me for a few minutes and then I signed off and was presented with my pay which amounted to £11-13s-0d (£11-65p) and one of my most prized possessions, my discharge certificate stating that I had served as A.B. aboard the four masted barque 'OLIVEBANK'. This was to me promotion indeed, and did much to help me in the years to come.

4-Masted Barque "OLIVEBANK,"
Gross 2795.   Nett 2427.

Mariehamn, FINLAND.

Port of _____

_____ *193*____

This is to certify that L. H. Townend has served onboard the Finnish 4:masted barque "Olivebank", as A. B., during a voyage from Glasgow to Port Victoria, South Australia, and back to Barry Dock via Queenstown, from October 15th 1938 to Aug. 5th 1939.

During his stay on board he has always acted in a strictly sober and good manner, always worked in the interest of the ship and the master, and has done his duties to my entire satisfaction. He is well recommended to anyone in need of his services. I wish him success.

Barry Dock Aug. 5th 1939.

Carl Granith

One of my most prized possessions

The Captain wished me well and offered me his hand which I was very proud to take and we said goodbye but not before he asked me to convey his regards to Geoff should I happen to see him.

I went out on deck and said my goodbyes to the three Mates (I was by now sorry even that I was parting company with Mr. Anderson, who really was a first rate man.)

I said my several goodbyes to all my old shipmates and picked up my gear and set off for the railway station. Borge Kulberg kindly humped some of my gear for me as he had to have something attended to by the Finnish Consul in Cardiff, where in fact I also had to go in order to have my certificate of discharge stamped.

We both presently boarded the train for Cardiff and as we ran parallel to the dock and watched old 'OLIVEBANK' until she was out of sight, I wondered if I would ever set eyes on her again.

Sadly it was not to be.

I had fulfilled one ambition at least. I had served in a big square rigger on a long haul. I had been lucky to have served under such a fine shipmaster and his three officers and shared all the dangers of the voyage with my shipmates and come out of it all unscathed and unhurt and I hope, a much wiser person. I had been in good hands.

We had not taken the Cape Horn road - this much I had missed, for I could only rate myself as half a shell back and I would so much have liked to have been a full blooded one but through force of circumstances this was not to be. The definition of a shell back is one who rounded Cape Horn in commercial sail and when having done that, one is accorded the right and the privilege, doubtful as the latter may be, of spitting up to windward whenever one feels so inclined.

As I bring this account of my voyage in 'OLIVEBANK' to a close I feel that it may be best to clarify what would appear to be rather odd compass courses which we from time to time had to steer. But, as one will know we had to some degree to go where the wind took us and therefore from time to time some of the courses I have noted down would be many points off the desired course, but would be the best heading we could make at any given time. The compass courses I have given were usually the ones given at the time I was at the wheel but in some cases they were the compass courses taken at noon, as were most of the ships positions.

The following few lines of verse pretty well sums up the life of the old windjammer men up to at least the turn of the century and probably into the early years of this century.

LUCK
What brings you, Sailor, home from the sea
Coffers of gold and of ivory?
When first I went to sea as a lad
A new Jack knife was all I had,
And I've sailed for Fifty years and three
To the coasts of gold and ivory,
And now at the end of a lucky life,
Well - still I've got my old Jack knife.

(Wilfred Gibson 1878)

I do not possess an old Jack knife, but I still have my old sou'wester, albeit not as good as it was after having suffered many gales in many climes but at least it still turns water. Purchased from a seaman's outfitter down the Govan Road, Glasgow in October 1938, price around 2/6d (12p) and manufactured by Barbours of South Shields. Surely a tribute to British Industry when they made sou'westers as they built ships – amongst the world's best.

So ends the account of my voyage on the

Sailing Vessel 'OLIVEBANK'

in the

Last Great Grain Race 1938/39.

EPILOGUE

'OLIVEBANK' completed discharging her cargo in Barry Docks South Wales and sailed from that Port for Finland on 28th or 29th of August, 1939.

At approx 14.00 hrs on Friday September 8th in 55' 53"N   05'07"E. she struck a German mine which tore out her bottom and she sank like a stone with the loss of 14 of her complement:

Captain Carl Granith
Chief Officer Ragnar Wuori
Steward Arne Stromberg
Cook Rolf Forsman
Sailmaker Niilo Kangas
Carpenter Kaiku Luotonen
Seaman Tor Sonntag
Seaman Alpo Alanen
Seaman Per Finneman
Seaman Unto Kanerva
Seaman Lennart Henriksson
Seaman Julius Henriksson
Seaman Arne Laakso
Seaman Valter Englund.

A costly price indeed to pay for a few thousand loaves of bread.

As far as I can ascertain 'OLIVEBANK' was the first neutral vessel to be sunk during the war of 1939/45.

At this time I was in Cardiff where I had just joined S.S. Scoresby on 6/9/39, when the sinking was reported, both over the radio and in the newspapers on I believe the 11th or 12th September.

I went to see the Pastor at the Scandinavian Seamens' Church to see if he had any news as to who had been lost and who had survived but at that time he had not. A day or two later we sailed for the River Plate with still no news of my lost shipmates.

After the war I was lucky enough to make contact by letter with Artur Blomquist, who by this time was a Pilot in Hango and in his first letter to me dated 2/3/52 he told me briefly of the sinking.

He stated that from the day they left Barry Dock they seemed to have bad luck. The wind was against them as they tried to beat up the English Channel, which took them four days and for much of this time they had to tack twice each watch. After four days of this they got a fair wind and set course for Gothenburg. The crew knew that hostilities had commenced but did not know of the German minefield.

'OLIVEBANK' struck a mine at about 1400hrs on Friday 8/9/39 which broke her in two. She settled onto the sea bottom in comparatively shallow water. It would appear that most of her top hamper carried away but the foremast up to the top mast doubling remained also the fore upper topsail yard which had cockbilled leaving one yardarm submerged and seemingly fouled up in what remained of the fore rigging and the other yardarm above sea level resembling a spar buoy.

The seven survivors swam to the upper topsail yard and scrambled onto the 3 or 4 metres of yard arm which remained above water. They managed to lash themselves to the yard with rope and had to remain in this position lashed and clinging on as best they could for some 44 hours with a very disturbed sea running for much of the time.

Through two long cold nights, for the North sea is never warm at nights once you get a little distance from the land, their plight and their suffering both mental and physical must have been extreme. Wet through, cold, having neither food or water, holding on as best they could, severely shocked at the suddenness of the tragic disaster and of seeing some of their shipmates perish. All this plus the mental anguish of not knowing if they were to be saved themselves.

While they were in this unhappy plight they sighted one steam ship a long way off and then a German plane which flew low overhead but ignored them completely.

Fortunately on Sunday morning 10/9/39 they were spotted and rescued by a Danish fisherman Captain Soren Hanson in the fishing vessel 'TALONA' and were taken to Esbjerg in Denmark.

The survivors were:

2nd Mate. Knut Anderson
3rd Mate. Olavi Pollonen
Seaman Artur Evert Blomquist
Seaman Albin Bjorkman
Seaman Gunnar Lindross
Seaman Borge Kulberg
Seaman Sam Johansson.

Fortunately two more crew members Artur Berndtson and Olav Forsten had paid off 'OLIVEBANK' shortly after I did in order to get home to Finland to be in time for the commencement of term at the navigation school.

According to Artur Blomquist in his account of the sinking he states that the 1st Mate Ragnar Wuori who was seen clinging to what appeared to be a life boat buoyancy tank, drifted away on it, unable, to get to the comparative safety of the rigging. The plight of the other seven being what it was meant they were in no position to render him any assistance.

It is now October 1984 - over 45 years since the disaster occurred and not one year has gone by, that I have not thought of my old shipmates many times, and always on the dates September 8th, 9th and 10th and again on our own armistice day Nov 11th my thoughts have been of them.

The years have come and gone and I have lost many old shipmates, both in peacetime and in war and I am much saddened by their passing, for fine men they all were and of many nationalities.

One of my saddest thoughts is of envisaging Ragnar Wuori that superb seaman, who on many occasions had travelled the Cape Horn Road, that tough smallish man, who had a twinkle in his eye, and the heart of an ox, drifting away to his doom unable to help himself and unable to be helped by any of his shipmates.

"The sea, cruel, kindly and deep is their grave.
The waves turbulent waters, their memorial."

The above lines are on the headstone of a grave in the churchyard at Canisbay, between Fort Mey and John-o-Groats.

I sincerely hope that I may be forgiven for taking a copy of the inscription that is on the headstone, but I feel it is most appropriate.

They are to the memory of a young Merchant Seaman who was lost in the North Atlantic during the war and I feel are a fitting epitaph to all of:

> *They that go down to the sea in ships*
> *That do business in great waters*
> *These see the works of the Lord*
> *And His wonders in the deep.*
>
> *(Psalm 107, verses 23,24).*

Since the war years I have heard that Mr. Anderson our 2nd Mate was lost at sea during the war and that Mr Pollonen our 3rd Mate died some years after the war. I understand Geoff Robertshaw saw him in Helsinki when the Olympic games were held there post war in 1952 but I cannot vouch for this.

In a letter from Artur Blomquist to me dated 12/12/52 he reports the tragic death of Sam Johansson in Oct 1952. Sam at this time was 1st Mate on the Finnish Motor vessel 'YVONNE' which unfortunately caught fire and poor Sam, during the course of his duties was very badly burned and died in hospital shortly afterwards.

In a further letter dated 26/9/54 also from Artur Blomquist I learn that Gunnar Lindross was in the evacuation of Dunkirk and was unlucky enough to lose a leg but was, at the time of writing, a taxi-driver in New York, surely a hazardous occupation to say the least.

Geoff Robertshaw died June 13th 1983 in his 73rd year. My wife and I were able to attend the funeral service at Mytholmroyd Church where Geoff was interred. The funeral service was conducted by the Rev. Jon Robertshaw, who is Geoff's nephew and was himself a Merchant seaman apprentice for several years before entering the church.

The service was very fitting and as can well be imagined, conducted in a most appropriate and seamanlike manner, for a seaman, by a seaman. The Rev. Jon is still closely connected to the sea as his living is down among the fisherfolk of Looe and Polperro.

I am happy to place on record that the church was full for the service. Jon had made a small cross out of driftwood, Kelp and sundry pieces of flotsam and jetsam which he had picked up on the beach in Cornwall. The small cross was placed on the coffin and lowered with it into the grave, which I feel would have given the old Cape Horner much satisfaction and indeed pleasure, had he known of its presence.

In the 'Cape Horner' Vol.2, No.4, January 1984, there is a very fitting obituary to Geoff which gives a brief account of his sea faring life, which the Rev. Jon prepared most adequately from extracts of Geoff's diaries.

Geoff followed the sea for several more years after his second voyage in 'OLIVEBANK' but unhappily he was discharged from further sea service 7/11/44 owing to a war disability, though I believe he did make one or two voyages in foreign flag vessels after this time. I used to visit him several times a year after I had 'come ashore' (as we lived only about 5 miles from each other).

On the last occasion that I paid him a visit just a few months before his death he was up aloft repairing his house roof. On his descending, I noticed that one hand and wrist were swathed in bandages. Enquiring as to what had happened, he said, "Oh, it is nothing Len, I was up the ladder last week clearing leaves from the easing trough and the bloody ladder slipped and I landed in the garden." A fall of about 20 feet. He informed me that getting up to his house roof did not present any great problems but he had misgivings as to whether he could make it up to a Royal yard as his rheumatism played him up from time to time.

I kept in touch with Miss Isabella Kiernander until she died. She was very upset by the loss of 'OLIVEBANK', for she had known Capt. Granith and the 1st Mate Ragnar Wuori and the sailmaker Niilo Kangas for several years.

In one letter to me she told me she had placed a wreath upon the sea down on the foreshore of her home in Worthing.

In the Sea Breezes column of the Journal of Commerce Oct 28th 1939 were two touching, articles to the memory of 'OLIVEBANK' and her Master and Crewmen that had perished. One was by Isabella and the other one by Geoff Robertshaw.

Isabella ends her tribute in this way:

> *'But maybe you sail, (and the wind is fair)*
> *On some great uncharted sea*
> *Where the sound of your laughter fills the air*
> *As you tack and wait for me.'*

I was sorry I never met Isabella again, for she was a lovely person.

Happily I still treasure her book of poems and also many more of her poems of the sea and ships and sailormen which do not appear in the book but which she sent me from time to time.

Artur Blomquist was the only other member of our old crew with whom I got in touch. He was chief Pilot at Hango for several years but I am sorry to say I lost contact this last few years. I am at this time (1984) endeavouring to once more get in touch.

For many years during my working life, both as a seaman and later as a long distance lorry driver I always tried, whenever I got into proximity with any Finnish vessel, to go and make enquiries as to whether any of my old shipmates were in the crew list. Unfortunately they never were, although I did get news (albeit old news) of both Blomquist and Kulberg from ships I visited in Bristol and Great Yarmouth.

I am pleased to report that during early July of 1984 I was in Finland (for the first time ever) and I made contact with my old shipmate and very good friend Albin Bjorkman and his wife and daughter. Albin like myself is now 67 years old and retired. He was for many years a Pilot at Vasa and now lives in the lovely coastal town of Kasko. He chose a lovely place for retirement for he can sit in his home and watch the ships pass by, not more than 75 yards from his window. He told me that after his retirement he signed on a Finnish vessel as 2nd Mate and made one last long voyage to East and West Africa and the Far East, which he had enjoyed.

I would say the years had treated him kindly for I would have known him even if I had run across him in some far-away place.

It was good to see him again and along with my wife and some Norwegian friends we rolled up at his home about 2145 on the 3/7/84 and were entertained right royally with coffee, strawberries and ice cream and whisky. Albin also presented me with a book (ALANDSKA SKEPPS - PORTRAIT I ORD OCH BILD, which interpreted is ALANDS SHIPS - PORTRAIT IN WORD AND PICTURE) by Lars Gronstrand. This book written in Swedish with a forward in English gives much coverage to the sailing vessels of Aland with many fine photo graphs, including two of 'OLIVEBANK' and one of the seven lads who survived.

Through Albin I was able to call the next day at the home of Borge Kulberg who lives in Abo. Unfortunately he was away but his wife was able to contact him on the phone and we had a pleasant few minutes chat. I understand he has written an account of his voyage in old 'OLIVEBANK' which I look forward to reading in due course.

As one travels through life, odd happenings and strange coincidences take place and one which happened to Geoff Robertshaw and myself (though at the time neither knew of the others involvement) may I feel be worth a mention.

During the period 14/2/40 until 23/2/44 I was serving in vessels of the Furness Withy fleet sailing out of Manchester. I was home on leave from M.V. 'PACIFIC EXPORTER' during Feb 1941 and on 2nd March I received a telegram from the Bosun, Tom Pepper, requesting me to be back on board the following day ready to sign articles.

On arriving back aboard I reported to the Bosun and told him I felt like a change of scenery to which he replied, "Well Len, we are having a change this trip, we are going to the Atlantic Coast of Canada not the Pacific shore but if you feel like a change pop over to the office and see if they have anything else to offer and meanwhile I will hold on to your job here until mid afternoon".

I went over to the Companies office on No. 8 Dock Salford and reported to Mr Bart Furse who in this day and age would be called the Company Personnel Officer and who was a very well respected figure in the Manchester Area shipping circle. This of course was early 1941 and several months before the formation of the Merchant Navy pool, when seamen were still treated as casual workers and still had freedom of choice regarding which companies or ships with which they preferred to seek employment. He had one A.B's job going in S.S.'SARDINIAN PRINCE' sailing that afternoon and he told me he had already sent one man down for the job but for some reason or other the A.B. had

160

reported back saying he did not want to sign on.

The arrangement was that I should go over to the 'SARDINIAN PRINCE' and present my discharge book to her Chief Officer for inspection and then come back and report to Mr Furse.

I went across the docks and went aboard and within a couple of minutes I decided not to go in her. I didn't even report to the Chief Officer but went back to Mr Furse at the office. Later in the day I signed articles once again aboard 'PACIFIC EXPORTER'.

In no way can I account for my behaviour on that day and I must add that I did not have any premonition of impending disaster. However, it was the last voyage of the S.S. 'SARDINIAN PRINCE' as she was intercepted by the 'SCHARNHORST' and sunk in 44°N 43°W on 16/3/41. To the best of my knowledge, all the crew was taken prisoner but I am not certain of this point.

I happened to relate this story to Geoff one evening in 1953 when my wife and I were paying a visit to his home and before I had even given any dates, he took up the story from me and by a strange coincidence it turned out that he had been the A.B. who turned down the job prior to me.

Geoff told me that he had felt or sensed that something was going to happen to the ship and decided he would not sail in her.

He later submitted this account to the Editor of World Wide Magazine which was subsequently published on pages 351 and 352 of the March 1954 issue. Unfortunately one or two minor errors appeared in the account, but other than mistakenly stating that I was currently serving in S.S.'MANCHESTER REGIMENT' which should have read M.V.'PACIFIC EXPORTER' any other mistakes were of a minor nature and the gist of the story was true. These errors were no fault of the Editor, but were mistakes made by Geoff in his report.

The 1938/39 Grain race proved to be the last as the war put an end for all time to this annual event.

It is true to say that Pamir, Passat and Viking did in fact bring one or two grain cargoes to Europe after hostilities ceased, but by this time there were very few square riggers left.

In this last race as far as I am aware 13 vessels took part ten of them were Finnish and owned by the Erikson line, one was Swedish, and two were German.

'MOSHULU' took 91 days.

'PAMIR' took 96 days.

'PADUA' took 98 days.

'PASSAT' took 98 days.

'KOMMODORE JOHNSEN' took 107 days.

'POMMERN' took 117 days

'OLIVEBANK' took 118 days.

'ABRAHAM RYDBERG' took 120 days.

'ARCHIBALD RUSSELL' took 121 days.

'VIKING' took 122 days.

'WINTERHUDE' took 134 days.

'KILLORAN' took 139 days.

'LAWHILL' took 140 days.

'Penang' did not participate and I cannot report on 'PRIWALL' as I am not sure of the movements of this vessel.

WHERE ARE THEY NOW

'KILLORAN', 'PENANG', and 'OLIVEBANK' were all war casualties.

'ARCHIBALD RUSSELL" was broken up on the Tyne after the war.

"PAMIR" was lost in 1957 with great loss of life. She was back under the German Flag and was employed as a cargo carrying training vessel.

"PASSAT" was employed in similar fashion but after the loss of "PAMIR" was withdrawn from sea service and as far as I know is still afloat in a German Port.

"PADUA" is now the Russian training ship "KRUZENSHTERN" and still sails the sea.

"MOSHULU" is in preservation in the U.S.A.

"VIKING" is in preservation in Gothenberg, Sweden.

'POMMERN" is in preservation in Mariehamn, Aland.

'ABRAHAM RYDBERG' became a training ship under the Portuguese Flag. The last time I saw her was in the Port of Calveston U.S.A. in 1947. By this time her appearance was spoilt as she was now a typical sea going training vessel, complete with extra deck houses and funnel. I do not know what became of her after that time.

'LAWHILL' I last saw her in a not too good condition in 1945 she appeared to be laid up either in Durban or Lorenco Marques - I think the former port. I believe she was eventually broken up.

'WINTERHUDE' was broken up.

A sad end indeed for most of those old vessels which were more or less the last of the many and as for myself I am proud to be the last privileged British sailor to have been lucky enough to be a crew member in that lovely old British built 4 Masted Barque 'OLIVEBANK' on her last voyage.

There used to be a saying amongst the old order of sailing ship men, "Anybody who went to sea from choice would go to Hell for a pastime". This I can well understand for in the old days the life of a foremast hand must have been a hard and bitter struggle against his fellow man and against the elements, with little in his belly and less in his pocket. His life must often have seemed hopeless and futile.

Not so with us younger seafarers who elected to follow the sea, for most of us younger windjammer men it was a high adventure. True, we still were up against the elements and we did not get much pay for our efforts, but it was a great training ground and for those who had the initiative, the drive and the ability and aimed their sights high enough, there was by the Grace of God nothing to stop them getting right to the top.

This was not the case regarding myself, as I was never much of a scholar and I suppose I was happier playing about with a bit of rope or up to my arm pits in a drum of red lead, fish oil and graphite or what have you. Albeit, I was happy with my lot and have no regrets.

Promotion came fairly rapidly during the war years, chiefly caused by war casualties and not by any particular ability on my part. I was lucky to be promoted to Bosun by March 1942 and at that time I was told I was the youngest Bosun sailing out of Manchester on a regular basis and I remained as Bosun all my seafaring days, with the exception of my time with the whalers.

The first poem in Isabella Kiernanders' book 'Songs of the Tall Ships' is dedicated to the Finnish four masted barque 'OLIVEBANK' and I feel is the best way of bringing the account of this voyage to a close.

THE SHIP LOVER

I love them all….these children of the sea:
The liner, with her vast and gleaming decks;
The squat and pompous tug; the ancient ketch;
The somber mystery of forgotten wrecks.

The dingy coal hulk,that was once a thing
Of loveliness and grace that sailed the seas;
The grimy collier beating home to port;
Some kind of beauty I can find in these.

The Medway barge, her rough brown sails a-dance;
The Grimsby trawler, toiling in the deep,
Sailing in storm, in fog, in bitter cold,
Wresting the sea's great harvest - while we sleep.

The cable ship - that link of lonely hearts...
A silent voice that calls across the seas;
The pleasure steamer, filled with joyous crowds,
Her music floating aft upon the breeze.

The lovely fishing smack, her coarse, patched sails
In russet harmony ' gainst evening skies;
The humble ferry boat, with human freight
As to and fro so patiently she plies.

The whaler, in her distant solitude,
Of frozen seas, and pale Antarctic snows,
A little world with ears astrain to catch
The look-out's voice from For'ard, "There she blows"!

The rusty tanker, riding lonely seas,
Her salt encrusted funnel raking aft;
The lonely lightship , watchman of the deep:
And all the multitude of smaller craft.

The majesty of dreadnoughts, wrapt in mist;
The lithe destroyers, speeding thro' the night;
The stately strength of cruisers - all the ships
That help to make, and keep, an Empire's might.

The sturdy salvage ships that lend a hand;
Old, little schooners, coastwise and deep sea;
The Mission ships; and those that chart the depths
Or tramp the sea's old roads... each calls to me...

All ships have beauty if you love them well,
But fairest are white wings that rake the sky,
The tall ships and the glory of the past:
Men realize beauty's dream ... to let it die...

Oh! best of all I love these white winged ships,
The tall, strong, splendour of a barque, home bound,
In her there dwells the beauty of all ships,
In her the magic of all seas is found.

FINAL WORDS

When the coal and the oil supplies become exhausted (as in time they surely must) and if once again the great windships sail the seas (as they may) and if there is such a thing as reincarnation (and I am selfish enough to hope that there is), then it would be my hope that I may reappear and for a time at least tramp round a capstan or take in a Royal on some black foul night with my old shipmates of yesteryear.

Looking into the future 1925 Bridlington